AN ANVIL ORIGINAL
Under the general editorship of Louis L. Snyder

BASIC DOCUMENTS ON THE CONFEDERATION AND CONSTITUTION

RICHARD B. MORRIS

Gouverneur Morris Professor of History, Columbia University
Editor, *Encyclopedia of American History*

VAN NOSTRAND REINHOLD COMPANY

New York   Cincinnati   Toronto   London   Melbourne

Van Nostrand Reinhold Company Regional Offices:
Cincinnati *New York* *Chicago* *Millbrae* *Dallas*

Van Nostrand Reinhold Company Foreign Offices:
London *Toronto* *Melbourne*

Copyright © 1970 by Litton Educational Publishing, Inc.

Published by Van Nostrand Reinhold Company
450 West 33rd Street, New York, N.Y. 10001

Published simultaneously in Canada by
D. Van Nostrand Company (Canada), Ltd.

10 9 8 7 6 5 4 3 2 1

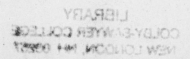

To
MY FELLOW LABORERS OVER THE YEARS
in the Vineyard of John Jay
with affection and appreciation

Preface

No half dozen years in American history are more crowded with critical events or more pregnant with constructive programs for improving the nation's posture abroad and at home, for putting its economic house in order, for initiating and digesting reforms, and for building the foundation blocks of a federal governmental system than the years 1783–1789.

If the American revolutionary era decided the question of how men made government, it also served as the testing ground for the proposition that a republic with severely limited powers could persuade thirteen fiercely independent states to subordinate their interests to the general good and, at the same time, demonstrate innovating statesmanship in governing the new territories which had been acquired at the peacemaking. The proposition that extensive powers could be conferred on a national government without jeopardizing the peoples' liberties, to secure which the Revolution had been waged, seemed especially dubious to some of those whose revolutionary ardor could not be impeached.

This documentary collection suggests that these questions were insistent ones from the moment the British troops evacuated American soil until the ratification of the Constitution and the adoption of a Bill of Rights. Almost to the end of the period under review, the resolution of these issues could not be confidently predicted. The documents assembled herein aim at clarifying the issues and presenting them through the eyes of those most intimately involved.

In the assembling of these documents, the editor is especially indebted to Professor Robert Dinkin, of Fresno State College, for many helpful suggestions and to Dr. Aleine Austin, of the University of Maryland at Baltimore, for leads to documents on the internal crisis in northern New England. For the preparation and collation of the text, acknowledgment must be made to Miss Ene Sirvet.

Richard B. Morris

Table of Contents

Introduction

The Confederation interlude in American history may properly be considered as both a continuation and fulfillment of movements touched off by the War for Independence and as a testing-ground of the political institutions of the new republic. This collection of documents seeks to probe and illumine both aspects of the period, the republic's prospects when peace came, its accomplishments and its shortcomings, and the men and events responsible for the adoption of the Federal Constitution.

To consider the American Revolution as terminating with the signing of the Definitive Peace Treaty of Paris on September 3, 1783, would be to confine that movement within narrow military boundaries. To achieve the gains of the Revolution and to move toward the goals that the Revolution enunciated constituted enormous tasks ahead. Enemy troops had to be evacuated, the West to be secured, the nation's economy to be rebuilt after eight years of savage warfare and widespread plunder, and the new government set up under the Articles of Confederation had to be put to the tests of peacetime operation.

How effective the Confederation government was in resolving these problems is the central issue raised by this book. Contemporaries themselves were divided on the question, as historians have been since then in reviewing those years. As for the Founding Fathers themselves, a majority saw the nation drifting toward anarchy. Wrote Washington in the fall of 1786, "I predict the worst consequences from a half-starved, limping government, always moving upon crutches and tottering at every step." Again he asserted: "I do not conceive we can long exist as a nation without having lodged somewhere a power which will pervade the whole Union in as energetic a manner as the authority of the State government extends over the several states."

Shays' Rebellion, which spread from interior Massachusetts to New Hampshire and Vermont (*see Documents 33, 34, 35*), understandably aroused the New England Federalists who were closest to the disturbing events, but others outside New England shared their perturbation. During the fall of 1786, John Jay, the Secretary for Foreign Affairs, kept writing Jefferson that "the inefficacy of our Government becomes daily more and more apparent," while Madison took up his pen to tell Jefferson of the "dangerous defects" in the Confederation. *The Federalist* papers (*Documents 48, 49*) present the classic contemporary view of the weakness of the Confederation and the need for a stronger central governmental structure. Hamilton was perhaps the most explicit, attacking the Confederation government as inefficient, asserting that the country had "reached almost the last stage of national humiliation," and disparaging "the present shadow of a federal government."

The statesmen of the Confederation who were involved with issues of a national or international character were in general agreement in attributing the obvious weaknesses of the Confederation to financial muddling by the states; to the dumping of English manufactured goods; to the loss of the British West Indian market; to paper money; to stay laws; to state tariffs; but, above all, to a lack of coercive power by a central authority. Observers in charge of foreign affairs, notably John Jay and John Adams, felt that this was the most critical spot in the American system of government. "I may reason till I die to no purpose," declared Adams in June 1785. "It is unanimity in America which will produce a fair treaty of commerce."

Conversely, state leaders, concerned about preserving that state sovereignty for which they felt the Revolution was fought and about maintaining their own power base, resented government encroachment upon their sources of revenue, such as tariffs, and were fearful of a strong central executive and a powerful central judiciary. Such leaders were much more complacent about conditions under the Confederation. Governor George Clinton of New York intimated that the calling of a Constitutional Convention was "calculated to impress the people with an idea of evils which do not exist." Mixed with fears of big central government and legitimate concern over the omission from the Federal Constitution of a bill of rights—concern shared by such notable Antifederalists as George Mason and Richard Henry Lee (*see Documents 46, 47*)—was a view expressed by other lesser Antifederalists, notably at the Pennsylvania ratifying convention, that state legislatures had been intimidated into calling state ratifying conventions by unfounded talk of impending anarchy.

This division of opinion in 1787 over the successes or failures of the Confederation interlude has continued down to the present day. How deep was the depression in the mid-eighties and when did it abate? Statistics are hardly reassuring to those who take a roseate view of the period. Commodity prices declined thirty percent between 1785 and 1789; farm wages fell to a low of forty cents a day by 1787; mortgage foreclosures and judgments for debt in central and western Massachusetts had by that year reached an all-time high; while in the Valley of Virginia executions more than doubled between 1784 and 1788. The only economic index that showed an upturn was that for foreign trade; in commerce the worst of the depression had set in a bit earlier than in other areas and had demonstrated a more complete recovery by 1788.

Nationalist historians and commentators of the Constitution throughout the nineteenth century portrayed the period as "critical" and spoke of "the contemptible impotence of Congress," but it was John Fiske's *The Critical Period in American History, 1783–1789* (first edition, 1888), which fastened upon this epoch a popular nomenclature that dies hard. There were occasional dissenting views. In 1871 Henry B. Dawson, a military historian, charged that the Federalists had conspired to falsify the true conditions of the period in a deliberate effort to create panic and undermine the government of the Confederation. Dawson had touched off certain doubts, which were again raised in 1907 by J. Allen Smith in his *The Spirit of American Government.* Therein it is argued that the entire absence of checks and balances in the Articles of Confederation (*see Document 4*) was a victory for the democratic forces and that the conservatives, once they had a chance to assess the situation, set about, in more or less conspiratorial fashion, to redress the balance.

Even earlier, in 1894, Orin G. Libby's *Geographical Distribution of the Vote of the Thirteen States on the Federal Constitution* demonstrated the role of sectionalism in ratification and showed how voters in seaport towns, along great rivers, and other arteries of interstate trade strongly supported the Constitution, while those in interior regions, less dependent on interstate or foreign trade, were heavily opposed. These new approaches to the adoption of the Constitution—the Turnerian of Libby with its stress on the role of social and economic areas, independent of state lines—and the class conflict approach of Dawson, J. Allen Smith, and others, profoundly influenced Charles A. Beard. In *An Economic Interpretation of the Constitution of the United*

States (1913), Beard defended the "critical period" as in fact not so critical after all, but "a phantom of the imagination produced by some undoubted evils which could have been remedied without a political revolution." Beard saw the advocates of the Constitution as the public security holders, the creditors, the seaboard financial and commercial interests, and the holders of personalty, while the opponents were debtors, agrarians, and holders of realty.

Beard's seminal work spawned a group of revisionist historians, who have devoted themselves to recounting the constructive measures taken in the Confederation period to repair federal and state finances. They have adduced evidence to demonstrate that the Confederation actually managed to reduce the principal of its debt and have presented in a favorable light the role of the states in paying off the national debt. They have pointed to the rapid amortization of state debts as evidence of the ability of the states to put their financial houses in order without much help from a central government, and they have shown conclusively that the states had now largely assumed the debt-funding role that the federal government had proved incapable of shouldering. If there was lawlessness in this period, it now appears to have been pretty much confined to a few sections of the country. In most states the forces of law and order never lost the upper hand. For example, in New York, Governor George Clinton personally led the troops of his state against the insurrectionary Shays. In most cases—and Maryland is an excellent example—the disgruntled elements confined their efforts to obtaining relief in a legal manner through legislative action.

Those who would sustain the conspiratorial thesis point to the Newburgh Address (*see Document 6*), which dramatized the nation's fiscal collapse. That default had triggered a cluster of measures transcending fiscal reform and aimed at recasting the structure of the Union. Although anticipated by young Alexander Hamilton, Robert Morris, the financier of the Revolution, was the prime mover and architect of the new fiscal edifice, aided and abetted by his associate Gouverneur Morris. In a far-reaching design for his Bank of North America, Morris embraced the intention of bringing about an early retirement of all federal and state currencies and replacing them with bank notes to tie the several states "more closely together in one general money connexion," as he put it in a letter to John Jay, penned in 1781, and "indissolubly to attach many powerful individuals to the cause of

our country by the strong principle of self-love and the immediate sense of private interest." As Superintendent of Finance,
Morris accomplished a good deal. He introduced the contract
system of supplying the army. He effected necessary economies
in the federal budget, and his bank provided the flexibility necessary to underwrite his complex fiscal operations. There soon arose
a group of nationalists about Morris who insisted that the debts,
both state and federal, should be paid only out of federal taxes,
levied and collected by Congress. This objective would necessitate
amending the Articles to provide Congress with the taxing power
it lacked. When Rhode Island, from motives of self-interest,
blocked the passage by Congress of an impost levy, Morris resigned.

With Congress hamstrung by the Articles of Confederation,
the initiative was seized by a group of discontented army officers
primed by an inner circle of army conservatives from the Morris
coterie. What they sought apparently was what would have
amounted to a *coup d'état* inside the framework of the Articles
of Confederation. In combination with the public creditors, the
army officers constituted a formidable group. But their plans
were smashed by Washington's refusal to put military pressure
on Congress or to lead a thinly veiled military coup. His courage-
ous disavowal of the Newburgh plot and his rebuke of the plotters (*see Document 7*) forced the creditors to look to the states
for the satisfaction of their claims. The conspiracy against the
Confederation, if it ever really existed, dissolved.

Even though the states continued to assume a goodly part of
the burden of the domestic debt, Congress continued to be fiscally
impotent. Confronted with the claims of foreign nations and
foreign debtors, Congress was obliged to default on its foreign
obligations in large part. After 1785 it failed to pay interest on
its Dutch loan, and it defaulted entirely on the contracts made
with the French government. In effect, by the year 1787 the national credit had virtually vanished and Congress was teetering
on the brink of bankruptcy. Critical though the moment, the
state of New York, which was enjoying considerable revenue
from its own imposts, in substance refused to concur in a new
proposal to grant the taxing power to Congress, very much as
had Rhode Island some years before. (*For New Jersey's position,
see Document 32.*)

It is in its conduct of foreign relations that the weakness of the
Congress of the Confederation is most evident. The United States,

counting on the dawning of a new economic era, had proffered to Europe a new scheme of commercial reciprocity, but only the Netherlands, Sweden, Prussia, and Morocco had given their virtually meaningless acceptance. Great Britain did not even deign to notice the proffer made in 1786 by John Adams and Thomas Jefferson. (*See Documents 22, 23.*) The United States could not assure the safety of its ships in the Mediterranean, nor could it secure from Spain a treaty opening up the vital artery, the Mississippi, to western settlers (*see Documents 24–26*). These failures in foreign affairs in the long run contributed more to the convoking of the Federal Convention in 1787 than the more immediate alarm over the course of Shays' Rebellion.

Recent investigators have demolished Beard's contention that the Constitution was slipped by or put over undemocratically in a society that was undemocratic, and that a *coup d'état* was effected by substantial holders of personal property as opposed to small farmers and debtors. It has been shown that slave owners, security holders, and holders of personalty also opposed the Constitution, while the Constitution numbered among its leading supporters men who did not own a single security. No one should minimize the depth of class feeling at this time or the comprehension by the Founding Fathers of their property interests, but as the Antifederalist leader Richard Henry Lee pointed out, "the weight of the community" comprised men of middling property, not in debt, and others "content with republican governments, and not aiming at immense fortunes, offices, and powers." Somehow or other the Federalists won over the support of a majority of this element, successfully persuading them that a strengthened and vitalized federal system was in the national interest.

Instead of regarding the adoption of the Constitution as the result of a counterrevolutionary movement, it can be argued that the vitalized federalism that it inaugurated and the tightening of the bonds of union that it effected precipitated a greater revolution in American life than did the separation of the Thirteen States from the Mother Country. Thus, the Confederation and Constitutional periods may properly be considered a continuation of the Revolutionary Age. The ratifying conventions may justifiably be regarded as revolutionary instruments of the people in the same sense that the ratifying convention that adopted the Massachusetts Constitution of 1780 proved a novel revolutionary mechanism for registering the consent of the government in establishing a new fundamental charter.

The Confederation interlude proved an extraordinary, if brief, period of testing. Prior to the adoption of the Federal Constitution, it was by no means certain that a republic could effectively govern a vast expanse of territory, deal as an equal with the great powers, allay sectional tensions, and silence secessionist murmurings. The inauguration of a creative constitutional era, by holding out a promise of resolving these issues, confounded the doubters and placed the national interest on a solid foundation.

BASIC DOCUMENTS ON THE
CONFEDERATION AND CONSTITUTION

Chapter I

THE CURTAIN GOES UP

Could a republic prove a viable system to administer a vast area of territory? Could the newly independent Thirteen States secure for themselves peace and prosperity? Out of his long experience in dealing with the army, with Congress, and with the Thirteen States, Washington, a sober realist, chose the occasion of a farewell Circular Letter addressed to the governors of the states, to stress the need for national purpose and for infusing the central government with greater energy and authority. As Washington saw it, for the United States to exist as an independent power the union of the states had to be "indissoluble" and "under one federal head"; the United States must display "a sacred regard to public justice"; adopt a "proper" peace establishment; and the people in turn must make the effort to transcend particularism and be willing to sacrifice individual advantage to the interest of the community. Washington's Circular Letter, in short, sets forth the minimum requirements for the establishment of an effective national government.

In the Mother Country, America's prospects were variously regarded. One of the more optimistic and friendly observers was Thomas Pownall, former royal governor of Massachusetts and a long-time authority on the American colonies. It was Pownall, a special adviser to England's Prime Minister, Lord Shelburne, who now promoted a program of liberalizing commerce with the former colonies. Shelburne himself had favored supplementing the Definitive Treaty of Peace with a commercial treaty based on the principle of free trade and had even looked forward to some kind of federal union based upon common economic advantages. A bill was accordingly drafted permitting American produce for the time being to enter British ports on the same footing as though British-owned, while treating American ships carrying such produce as those of other foreign states. During this interim period the bill would have permitted American ships to carry American goods to British colonies and islands

1

in America and to export any goods whatsoever from such British possessions. Duties and charges would in both cases be the same as for British-owned merchandise, transported by British ships and crews. However, by the time the bill came up in Parliament, Shelburne was already out of office and the younger Pitt, his successor, proved a lukewarm advocate.

The chief arguments against liberalizing trade with America were advanced by Lord Sheffield, whose Observations on the Commerce of the American States *marshaled an imposing array of statistics to support the argument that Americans must be treated as foreigners and not permitted to enjoy those branches of the carrying trade with the Empire in which they had previously participated, notably the trade in foodstuffs and timber with the British West Indies. Indeed, the American Revolution, to Lord Sheffield, was no calamity to England, as it would give Britain the opportunity of regaining the British West Indian carrying trade, while at the same time the British would continue to be the main supplier of manufacturers to the Americans, and British-owned ships the main carriers of such cargoes. The interest groups who espoused Sheffield's arguments against trade liberalization with America won the day. An Order in Council issued on July 2, 1783, barred American ships from the West Indian trade, and no commercial treaty was adopted. Instead, rivalry and exclusion ruled in place of cooperation and economic integration.*

1. George Washington's Last Circular Letter to the States, June 8, 1783*

Head-Quarters, Newburg,
8 June, 1783.

Sir,

The great object, for which I had the honor to hold an appointment in the service of my country, being accomplished, I am now preparing to resign it into the hands of Congress, and to return to that domestic retirement, which, it is well known, I left with the greatest reluctance; a retirement for which I have never ceased to sigh, through a long and painful absence, and in which (remote from the noise and trouble of the world) I meditate to pass the remainder of life, in a state of undisturbed repose. But before I carry this resolution into effect, I think it a duty incumbent on me to make this my last official communication; to congratulate you on the glorious events which Heaven has been pleased to produce in our favor; to offer my sentiments respecting some important subjects, which appear to me to be intimately connected with the tranquillity of the United States; to take my leave of your Excellency as a public character; and to give my final blessing to that country, in whose service I have spent the prime of my life, for whose sake I have consumed so many anxious days and watchful nights, and whose happiness, being extremely dear to me, will always constitute no inconsiderable part of my own.

Impressed with the liveliest sensibility on this pleasing occa-

* Worthington C. Ford (ed.), *The Writings of George Washington*, 14 vols. (New York, 1891), X, 254–265.

sion, I will claim the indulgence of dilating the more copiously on the subjects of our mutual felicitation. When we consider the magnitude of the prize we contended for, the doubtful nature of the contest, and the favorable manner in which it has terminated, we shall find the greatest possible reason for gratitude and rejoicing. This is a theme that will afford infinite delight to every benevolent and liberal mind, whether the event in contemplation be considered as the source of present enjoyment, or the parent of future happiness; and we shall have equal occasion to felicitate ourselves on the lot which Providence has assigned us, whether we view it in a natural, a political, or moral point of light.

The citizens of America, placed in the most enviable condition, as the sole lords and proprietors of a vast tract of continent, comprehending all the various soils and climates of the world, and abounding with all the necessaries and conveniences of life, are now, by the late satisfactory pacification, acknowledged to be possessed of absolute freedom and independency. They are, from this period, to be considered as the actors on a most conspicuous theatre, which seems to be peculiarly designated by Providence for the display of human greatness and felicity. Here they are not only surrounded with every thing, which can contribute to the completion of private and domestic enjoyment; but Heaven has crowned all its other blessings, by giving a fairer opportunity for political happiness, than any other nation has ever been favored with. Nothing can illustrate these observations more forcibly, than a recollection of the happy conjuncture of times and circumstances, under which our republic assumed its rank among the nations. The foundation of our empire was not laid in the gloomy age of ignorance and superstition; but at an epocha when the rights of mankind were better understood and more clearly defined, than at any former period. The researches of the human mind after social happiness have been carried to a great extent; the treasures of knowledge, acquired by the labors of philosophers, sages, and legislators, through a long succession of years, are laid open for our use, and their collected wisdom may be happily applied in the establishment of our forms of government. The free cultivation of letters, the unbounded extension of commerce, the progressive refinement of manners, the growing liberality of sentiment, and, above all, the pure and benign light of Revelation, have had a meliorating influence on mankind and increased the blessings of society. At this auspicious period, the United States came into existence as a nation; and, if their citizens should not be completely free and happy, the fault will be entirely their own.

Such is our situation, and such are our prospects; but notwithstanding the cup of blessing is thus reached out to us; notwithstanding happiness is ours, if we have a disposition to seize the occasion and make it our own; yet it appears to me there is an option still left to the United States of America, that it is in their choice, and depends upon their conduct, whether they will be respectable and prosperous, or contemptible and miserable, as a nation. This is the time of their political probation; this is the moment when the eyes of the whole world are turned upon them; this is the moment to establish or ruin their national character for ever; this is the favorable moment to give such a tone to our federal government, as will enable it to answer the ends of its institution, or this may be the ill-fated moment for relaxing the powers of the Union, annihilating the cement of the confederation, and exposing us to become the sport of European politics, which may play one State against another, to prevent their growing importance, and to serve their own interested purposes. For, according to the system of policy the States shall adopt at this moment, they will stand or fall; and by their confirmation or lapse it is yet to be decided, whether the revolution must ultimately be considered as a blessing or a curse; a blessing or a curse, not to the present age alone, for with our fate will the destiny of unborn millions be involved.

With this conviction of the importance of the present crisis, silence in me would be a crime. I will therefore speak to your Excellency the language of freedom and of sincerity without disguise. I am aware, however, that those who differ from me in political sentiment, may perhaps remark, I am stepping out of the proper line of my duty, and may possibly ascribe to arrogance or ostentation, what I know is alone the result of the purest intention. But the rectitude of my own heart, which disdains such unworthy motives; the part I have hitherto acted in life; the determination I have formed, of not taking any share in public business hereafter; the ardent desire I feel, and shall continue to manifest, of quietly enjoying, in private life, after all the toils of war, the benefits of a wise and liberal government, will, I flatter myself, sooner or later convince my countrymen, that I could have no sinister views in delivering, with so little reserve, the opinions contained in this address.

There are four things, which, I humbly conceive, are essential to the well-being, I may even venture to say, to the existence of the United States, as an independent power.

First.   An indissoluble union of the States under one federal head.

Secondly.   A sacred regard to public justice.

Thirdly.   The adoption of a proper peace establishment; and,

Fourthly.   The prevalence of that pacific and friendly disposition among the people of the United States, which will induce them to forget their local prejudices and policies; to make those mutual concessions, which are requisite to the general prosperity; and, in some instances, to sacrifice their individual advantages to the interest of the community.

These are the pillars on which the glorious fabric of our independency and national character must be supported. Liberty is the basis; and whoever would dare to sap the foundation, or overturn the structure, under whatever specious pretext he may attempt it, will merit the bitterest execration, and the severest punishment, which can be inflicted by his injured country.

On the three first articles I will make a few observations, leaving the last to the good sense and serious consideration of those immediately concerned.

Under the first head, although it may not be necessary or proper for me, in this place, to enter into a particular disquisition on the principles of the Union, and to take up the great question which has been frequently agitated, whether it be expedient and requisite for the States to delegate a larger proportion of power to Congress, or not; yet it will be a part of my duty, and that of every true patriot, to assert without reserve, and to insist upon, the following positions. That, unless the States will suffer Congress to exercise those prerogatives they are undoubtedly invested with by the constitution, every thing must very rapidly tend to anarchy and confusion. That it is indispensable to the happiness of the individual States, that there should be lodged somewhere a supreme power to regulate and govern the general concerns of the confederated republic, without which the Union cannot be of long duration. That there must be a faithful and pointed compliance, on the part of every State, with the late proposals and demands of Congress, or the most fatal consequences will ensue. That whatever measures have a tendency to disslove the Union, or contribute to violate or lessen the sovereign authority, ought to be considered as hostile to the liberty and independency of America, and the authors of them treated accordingly. And lastly, that unless we can be enabled, by the concurrence of the States, to participate of the fruits of the revolution, and enjoy the essential benefits of civil society, under a form of government so free and uncorrupted, so happily guarded against the danger of oppression, as has been devised and adopted by the articles of confederation, it will be a subject of regret, that so much blood and treasure have been lavished for no purpose, that so many sufferings have been encountered without a compensation, and that so many sacrifices have been made in vain.

Many other considerations might here be adduced to prove, that, without an entire conformity to the spirit of the Union, we cannot exist as an independent power. It will be sufficient for my purpose to mention but one or two, which seem to me of the greatest importance. It is only in our united character, as an empire, that our independence is acknowledged, that our power can be regarded, or our credit supported, among foreign nations. The treaties of the European powers with the United States of America will have no validity on a dissolution of the Union. We shall be left nearly in a state of nature; or we may find, by our own unhappy experience, that there is a natural and necessary progression from the extreme of anarchy to the extreme of tyranny, and that arbitrary power is most easily established on the ruins of liberty, abused to licentiousness.

As to the second article, which respects the performance of public justice, Congress have, in their late address to the United States, almost exhausted the subject; they have explained their ideas so fully, and have enforced the obligations the States are under, to render complete justice to all the public creditors, with so much dignity and energy, that, in my opinion, no real friend to the honor of independency of America can hesitate a single moment, respecting the propriety of complying with the just and honorable measures proposed. If their arguments do not produce conviction, I know of nothing that will have greater influence: especially when we recollect, that the system referred to, being the result of the collected wisdom of the continent, must be esteemed, if not perfect, certainly the least objectionable of any that could be devised; and that, if it shall not be carried into immediate execution, a national bankruptcy, with all its deplorable consequences, will take place, before any different plan can possibly be proposed and adopted. So pressing are the present circumstances, and such is the alternative now offered to the States.

The ability of the country to discharge the debts, which have been incurred in its defence, is not to be doubted; an inclination, I flatter myself, will not be wanting. The path of our duty is plain before us; honesty will be found, on every experiment, to be the best and only true policy. Let us then, as a nation, be just; let us fulfil the public contracts, which Congress had undoubtedly a right to make for the purpose of carrying on the war, with the same good faith we suppose ourselves bound to perform our private engagements. In the mean time, let an attention to the cheerful performance of their proper business, as individuals and as members of society, be earnestly inculcated on the citizens of America; then will they strengthen the hands of government, and be happy under its protection; every one will reap the fruit of his labors, every one will enjoy his own acquisitions, without molestation and without danger.

In this state of absolute freedom and perfect security, who will grudge to yield a very little of his property to support the common interest of society, and insure the protection of government? Who does not remember the frequent declarations, at the commencement of the war, that we should be completely satisfied, if, at the expense of one half, we could defend the remainder of our possessions? Where is the man to be found, who wishes to remain indebted for the defence of his own person and property to the exertions, the bravery, and the blood of others, without making one generous effort to repay the debt of honor and gratitude? In what part of the continent shall we find any man, or body of men, who would not blush to stand up and propose measures purposely calculated to rob the soldier of his stipend, and the public creditor of his due? And were it possible, that such a flagrant instance of injustice could ever happen, would it not excite the general indignation, and tend to bring down upon the authors of such measures the aggravated vengeance of Heaven? If, after all, a spirit of disunion, or a temper of obstinacy and perverseness should manifest itself in any of the States; if such an ungracious disposition should attempt to frustrate all the happy effects that might be expected to flow from the Union; if there should be a refusal to comply with the requisition for funds to discharge the annual interest of the public debts; and if that refusal should revive again all those jealousies, and produce all those evils, which are now happily removed, Congress, who have, in all their transactions, shown a great degree of magnanimity and justice, will stand justified in the sight of God and man; and the State alone, which puts itself in opposition to the aggregate wisdom of the continent, and follows such mistaken and pernicious counsels, will be responsible for all the consequences.

For my own part, conscious of having acted, while a servant of the public, in the manner I conceived best suited to promote the real interests of my country; having, in consequence of my fixed belief, in some measure pledged myself to the army, that their country would finally do them complete and ample justice; and not wishing to conceal any instance of my official conduct from the eyes of the world, I have thought proper to transmit to your Excellency the enclosed collection of papers, relative to the half-pay and commutation granted by Congress to the officers of the army. From these communications, my decided sentiments will be clearly comprehended, together with the conclusive reasons which induced me, at an early period, to recommend the adoption of this measure, in the most earnest and serious manner. As the proceedings of Congress, the army, and myself, are open to all, and contain, in my opinion, sufficient information to remove the prejudices and errors, which may have been entertained by any, I think it unnecessary to say anything more than just to observe, that the resolutions of Congress, now alluded to, are undoubtedly as absolutely binding upon the United States, as the most solemn acts of confederation or legislation.

As to the idea, which, I am informed, has in some instances prevailed, that the half-pay and commutation are to be regarded merely in the odious light of a pension, it ought to be exploded for ever. That provision should be viewed, as it really was, a reasonable compensation offered by Congress, at a time when they had nothing else to give to the officers of the army for services then to be performed. It was the only means to prevent a total dereliction of the service. It was a part of their hire. I may be allowed to say, it was the price of their blood, and of your independency: it is therefore more than a common debt, it is a debt of honor; it can never be considered as a pension or gratuity, nor be cancelled until it is fairly discharged.

With regard to a distinction between officers and soldiers, it is sufficient that the uniform experience of every nation of the world, combined with our own, proves the utility and propriety of the discrimination. Rewards, in proportion to the aids the public derives from them, are unquestionably due to all its servants. In some lines, the soldiers have perhaps generally had as ample a compensation for their services, by the large bounties which have been paid to them, as their officers will receive in the proposed commutation; in others, if, besides the donation of lands, the payment of arrearages of clothing and wages (in which articles all the component parts of the army must be put upon the same footing), we take into the estimate the douceurs many of the soldiers have received, and the gratuity of one year's full pay, which is promised to all, possibly their situation (every circumstance being duly considered) will not be deemed less eligible than that of the officers. Should a further reward, however, be judged equitable, I will venture to assert, no one will enjoy greater satisfaction than myself, on seeing an exemption, from taxes for a limited time, (which has been petitioned for in some instances,) or any other adequate immunity or compensation granted to the brave defenders of their country's cause; but neither the adoption or rejection of this proposition will in any manner affect, much less militate against, the act of Congress, by which they have offered five years' full pay, in lieu of the half-pay for life, which had been before promised to the officers of the army.

Before I conclude the subject of public justice, I cannot omit to mention the obligations this country is under to that meritorious class of veteran non-commissioned officers and privates, who have been discharged for inability, in consequence of the resolution of Congress of the 23d of April, 1782, on an annual pension for life. Their peculiar sufferings, their singular merits, and claims to that provision, need only be known, to interest all the feelings of humanity in their behalf. Nothing but a punctual payment of their annual allowance can rescue them from the most complicated misery; and nothing could be a more melancholy and distressing sight, than to behold those, who have shed their blood or lost their limbs in the service of their country, without a shelter, without a friend, and without the means of obtaining any of the necessaries or comforts of life, compelled to beg their daily bread from door to door. Suffer me to recommend those of this description, belonging to your State, to the warmest patronage of your Excellency and your legislature.

It is necessary to say but a few words on the third topic which was proposed, and which regards particularly the defence of the republic; as there can be little doubt but Congress will recommend a proper peace establishment for the United States, in which a due attention will be paid to the importance of placing the militia of the Union upon a regular and respectable footing. If this should be the case, I would beg leave to urge the great advantage of it in the strongest terms. The militia of this country must be considered as the palladium of our security, and the first effectual resort in case of hostility. It is essential, therefore, that the same system should pervade the whole; that the formation and discipline of the militia of the continent should be absolutely uniform, and that the same species of arms, accoutrements, and military apparatus, should be introduced in every part of the United States. No one, who has not learned it from experience, can conceive the difficulty, expense, and confusion, which result from a contrary system, or the vague arrangements which have hitherto prevailed.

If, in treating of political points, a greater latitude than usual has been taken in the course of this address, the importance of the crisis, and the magnitude of the objects in discussion, must be my apology. It is, however, neither my wish or expectation, that the preceding observations should claim any regard, except so far as they shall appear to be dictated by a good intention, consonant to the immutable rules of justice, calculated to produce a liberal system of policy, and founded on whatever experience may have been acquired by a long and close attention to public business. Here I might speak with the more confidence, from my actual observations; and, if it would not swell this letter (already too prolix) beyond the bounds I had prescribed to myself, I could demonstrate to every mind open to conviction, that in less time, and with much less expense, than has been incurred, the war might have been brought to the same happy conclusion, if the resources of the continent could have been properly drawn forth; that the distresses and disappointments, which have very often occurred, have, in too many instances, resulted more from a want of energy in the Continental government, than a deficiency of means in the particular States; that the inefficacy of measures arising from the want of an adequate authority in the supreme power, from a partial compliance with the requisitions of Congress in some of the States, and from a failure of punctuality in others, while it tended to damp the zeal of those, which were more willing to exert themselves, served also to accumulate the expenses of the war, and to frustrate the best concerted plans; and that the discouragement occasioned by the complicated difficulties and embarrassments, in which our affairs were by this means involved, would have long ago produced the dissolution of any army, less patient, less virtuous, and less persevering, than that which I have had the honor to command. But, while I mention these things, which are notorious facts, as the defects of our federal constitution, particularly in the prosecution of a war, I beg it may be understood, that, as I have ever taken a pleasure in gratefully acknowledging the assistance and support I have derived from every class of citizens, so shall I always be happy to do justice to the unparalleled exertions of the individual States on many interesting occasions.

I have thus freely disclosed what I wished to make known, before I surrendered up my public trust to those who committed it to me. The task is now accomplished. I now bid adieu to your

Excellency as the chief magistrate of your State, at the same time I bid a last farewell to the cares of office, and all the employments of public life.

It remains, then, to be my final and only request, that your Excellency will communicate these sentiments to your legislature at their next meeting, and that they may be considered as the legacy of one, who has ardently wished, on all occasions, to be useful to his country, and who, even in the shade of retirement, will not fail to implore the Divine benediction upon it.

I now make it my earnest prayer, that God would have you, and the State over which you preside, in his holy protection; that he would incline the hearts of the citizens to cultivate a spirit of subordination and obedience to government; to entertain a brotherly affection and love for one another, for their fellow citizens of the United States at large, and particularly for their brethren who have served in the field; and finally, that he would most graciously be pleased to dispose us all to do justice, to love mercy, and to demean ourselves with that charity, humility, and pacific temper of mind, which were the characteristics of the Divine Author of our blessed religion, and without an humble imitation of whose example in these things, we can never hope to be a happy nation.

I have the honor to be, with much esteem and respect, Sir, your Excellency's most obedient and most humble servant.

2.   A Call to Greatness: Thomas Pownall's *A Memorial Addressed to the Sovereigns of America*, 1783 *

It is not sufficient that the UNITED STATES feel that they are Sovereign; it is not sufficient that the sense of this is universally felt in America; it is not sufficient that they are conscious to themselves that the *Punctum Saliens,* the Source and Spring of the Activity of this Sovereign power, is within their System: until they *lift up on high a Standard to the Nations,* it will remain as an abstract idea, as a Theory in the World at large. This Sovereign must come forward amongst the Nations, as an active Existing Agent, a Personal Being, standing on the same ground as all other Personal Sovereigns. Its Powers, Commissions, Officers Civil and Military; its claims to, and its exercise of, the Rights of the Law of Nations, must have their full and free scope in act and deed: wherever they come forward, their Standard and Flag, the Ensign of the Majesty of their Sovereignty, must be erected, and its rights and privileges established amongst the Nations of the Earth; it must be acknowledged; respected; and, in all cases whatsoever, *treated as what it is,* the Actual Signal of a Sovereign Empire.

Being thus planted in a New System in a New Country; growing up under such principles of Truth and Nature; established in such a Constitution of Government; having in so short a period been brought forward to Independence, and become Sovereigns acknowledged so by the Sovereigns of Europe; all this coming into Event by Something beyond the ordinary course

* Thomas Pownall, *A Memorial Addressed to the Sovereigns of America* (London, 1783).

of Events in human affairs, THE UNITED STATES AND
CITIZENS OF AMERICA may say, *'It is the Lord's doings."*
But let them remember, that enjoying a System of police that
gives activity to their powers; that inhabiting a New World, a
land of plenty and liberty; a country which hath so many sources
of enjoyments which it offers to the Old World—let them remember the obligations which Heaven hath thus laid on them,
and the returns which this Goodness reclaims of them; that They
respect the rights and liberties of Mankind; that by a free commerce they diffuse to the World at large the surplus portion of
these good things which they must be continually creating in
their own World; that they consider themselves as the means in
the hands of Providence, of extending the Civilization of human
Society; and the Teachers, by their example, of those Political
Truths, which are meant, not to enslave, but to render men more
free and happy under Government. If they take up this Character within themselves, and hold out its operations and effect to
the Old World, they will become a Nation *to whom all Nations
will come;* a Power whom all the Powers of Europe will court
to Civil and Commercial Alliances; a People to whom the Remnants of all ruined People will fly, whom all the oppressed and
injured of every nation will seek to for refuge. *The riches of the
Sea will pour in upon them; the wealth of Nations must flow
in upon them;* and they must be a populous and Rich People.

3.   The Economy's Reliance on Great Britain: Lord Sheffield's *Observations On the Commerce of the American States*, 1783 *

At least four-fifths of the importations from Europe into the American States, were at all times made upon credit; and undoubtedly the States are in greater want of credit at this time than at former periods. It can be had only in Great Britain. The French who gave them credit, are all bankrupts: French merchants cannot give much credit. The Dutch in general have not trusted them to any amount; those who did have suffered; and it is not the custom of the Dutch to give credit, but on the best security. It is therefore obvious from this and the foregoing state of imports and exports, into what channels the commerce of the American States must inevitably flow, and that nearly four-fifths of their importations will be from Great Britain directly. Where articles are nearly equal, the superior credit afforded by England will always give the preference. The American will, doubtless, attempt to persuade the British merchant to be his security with foreigners; but it is certain many foreign articles will go to America through Great Britain, as formerly, on account of the difficulty the American merchant would find in resorting to every quarter of the world to collect a cargo. The Americans send ships to be loaded with all sorts of European goods. A general cargo for the American market cannot be made up on such advantageous terms in any part of the world as in England. In our ports, all articles may be got with dispatch—a most winning circumstance in trade; but wherever they carry fish, and those

* Lord Sheffield, *Observations on the Commerce of the American States* (London, 1784), 183–207, 263–264, 272.

articles for which England cannot be the entrepot, they will take back wine, silk, oil, &c. from Spain and Portugal, and the Mediterranean. But if we maintain the carrying trade, half the commerce of the American States, or less than half, without the expence of their government and protection, and without the extravagance of bounties, would be infinitely better for us than the monopoly, such as it was. . . .

What was foretold in the first edition of this work, has now [1784] actually happened. Every account from America says, that British manufactures are selling at a considerable profit, while other European goods cannot obtain the first cost. Every day's experience shews, that this country, from the nature and quality of its manufactures, and from the ascendancy it has acquired in commerce, will command three-fourths of the American trade. The American merchants solicit a correspondence, and beg for credit, because, while they feel their own want of capital, they know that our traders are more liberal, and our goods cheaper and better, than any in Europe. And the only danger is, not that the American merchants will ask for too few manufactures, but that they will obtain too many. The American consumers have been impoverished by an expensive war, which has bequeathed them many taxes to pay; and they will not be more punctual in their remittances at a time when they are associating against the payment of old debts. It may be for our interest to run some hazard, however, at the renewal of our correspondence, by accepting a trade which is pressed upon us by willing customers. But how far it may be prudent for the British merchant to comply with orders, till the several States hold out some regulations, that will give them security, is a question. . . .

It is well known, that numbers of our merchants have been made bankrupts through the bad payment of the Americans.

We are told it is proper to court the trade with the American states.

Their treaties with France and Holland, in direct terms, forbid our being put on a better footing than those countries. The state of our manufactures make it unnecessary; and, in general, nothing can be more weak than the idea of courting commerce. America will have from us what she cannot get cheaper and better elsewhere, and she will sell to us what we want from her as cheap as she will to others. . . . The truth is, we want little of her produce in Great-Britain, coarse tobacco excepted. The finest tobacco grows in the islands, and in South America. The indigo of the islands and of South America is infinitely better than that of North America, but we must take that and naval stores, and other articles from the American States which may be got as good or better elsewhere, in return for our manufactures, instead of money. In payment, for want of other sufficient returns, large quantities of tobacco must come to Great-Britain, and we can afford to give the best price for it, by taking it in exchange for our manufactures. . . .

Instead of exaggerating the loss suffered by the dismemberment of the empire, our thoughts may be employed to more advantage in considering what our situation really is, and the greatest advantage that can be derived from it. It will be found better than we expect, nor is the independence of the American States, notwithstanding their connection with France, likely to interfere with us so essentially as has been apprehended, except as to the carrying trade, the nursery for seamen. The carriage of our produce is nothing in comparison with that of America; a few tobacco ships will carry back as much of our manufactures as all the American States will consume. We must therefore retain the carrying trade wherever we possibly can.—But the demand for our manufactures will continually increase with the population of America. Those who have been disposed to despond may comfort themselves with the prospect, that if the American States should hereafter be able to manufacture for themselves, as the consumption of the manufactures of England decreases with them, the demand will encrease elsewhere; . . .

If manufacturers should emigrate from Europe to America, at least nine-tenths will become farmers; they will not work at manufactures when they can get double the profit by farming.

No American articles are so necessary to us, as our manufactures, &c., are to the Americans, and almost every article of the produce of the American States, which is brought into Europe, we may have at least as good and as cheap, if not better, elsewhere. Both as a friend and an enemy America has been burthensome to Great Britain. It may be some satisfaction to think, that by breaking off rather prematurely, Great Britain may find herself in a better situation in respect to America, than if she had fallen off when more ripe. . . .

It will not be an easy matter to bring the American States to act as a nation; they are not to be feared as such by us. It must be a long time before they can engage, or will concur in any material expence. A Stamp act, a Tea act, or such act that never can again occur, could alone unite them; their climate, their staples, their manners, are different; their interests opposite; and that which is beneficial to one is destructive to the other. In short, every circumstance proves that it will be extreme folly to enter into any engagements, by which we may not wish to be bound hereafter. It is impossible to name any material advantage the American States will, or can give us in return, more than what we of course shall have. No treaty can be made with the American States that can be binding on the whole of them. The act of Confederation does not enable Congress to form more than general treaties: at the moment of the highest authority of Congress the power in question was withheld by the several States. No treaty that could be made would suit the different interests. When treaties are necessary, they must be made with the States separately. Each State has reserved every power relative to imports, exports, prohibitions, duties, &c., to itself. But no treaty at present is necessary.

Chapter II

THE CONSTITUTIONAL AND LEGAL BASES OF THE NEW NATION

Two legal documents determined the character of the new nation. These were the Articles of Confederation, which laid down a plan of union, and the Definitive Treaty of Peace of 1783, by which Great Britain conceded independence to the Thirteen States. A draft of the Articles was presented to Congress by a committee headed by John Dickinson back in July of 1776, and for over a year the Articles were debated intermittently.

When finally approved the Articles were but a shadow of Dickinson's draft. Instead of broad powers being granted Congress, an article was inserted reserving sovereignty and independence to the several states. Three controversial features of the original draft were all resolved in favor of state authority. As in the original draft, the states were given one vote apiece in the Congress. Dickinson's draft provided for raising money by assigning quotas to the state governments, rather than by giving Congress power to levy and collect taxes directly. Dickinson would have assigned quotas on the basis of population which New England favored, but the South, where land was cheap, prevailed and in the final Articles the levying of requisitions on states was changed from population to land. Dickinson's committee would have conferred upon Congress the power over western lands, but that power was dropped altogether.

In this emasculated form, the Articles were formally adopted on November 15, 1777, and then submitted to each state for prompt ratification. Virginia was the first to ratify unconditionally; New York soon followed; and after seven months all but four states had ratified, with or without proposing amendments. Soon Georgia, Delaware, and New Jersey joined the ratifiers, but Maryland refused to ratify until the states claiming western lands ceded them to the United States. A great battle over the issue of the control and disposition of the public lands ensued, but finally the states with western land-claims complied—Virginia being the last on January 2, 1781. Maryland then signed the Articles on February 27th. Final ratification took place on March 1st, and the next day Congress assumed a new title, "The United States in Congress Assembled," with the president of the old Congress, Samuel Huntington, continuing in office. The Articles revealed that the states were not ready as yet to confer upon a federal government a strong executive authority or an effective taxing power. The legislative power of Congress was hamstrung by the provision requiring nine states to assent to major legislation or treaties, and the possibility of strengthening the fabric of union was dimmed by the provision that amendments to the Articles needed the approval not only of Congress but also the unanimous ratification of every state.

The American peacemakers in Paris—Benjamin Franklin, John Adams, and John Jay, with Henry Laurens joining them at the very last moment—capitalized on the factors of time and distance to act on their own initiative by negotiating a preliminary treaty with Great Britain separately from France despite explicit instructions of Congress to follow the advice of the King of France. Except for a separate and secret article on West Florida which was added to the Preliminaries but omitted from the Definitive Treaty (since Spain recovered the Floridas by her own treaty with Great Britain), the Definitive Treaty was identical with the Preliminary Articles signed on November 30, 1782. The treaty's most important clauses were those in which Great Britain recognized the independence of the Thirteen United States and conceded to the new nation a continental domain extending from the middle of the Great Lakes south to the 31st parallel and west to the Mississippi River.

On a few points the American commissioners arrived at compromises with their British counterparts to secure a mutually acceptable treaty, and these articles proved to be a subject of contention in the years of the Confederation and in some instances for more than a decade thereafter. There was first of all a northeastern boundary compromise, the acceptance of the *vaguely defined "St. Croix River" dividing Maine and Nova Scotia. Secondly, the United States was given the "right" to fish in their accustomed grounds off Newfoundland, the Grand Bank, and the Gulf of St. Lawrence, and the "liberty" to dry and cure fish on any unsettled shore on Labrador, the Magdalen Islands, and Nova Scotia so long as these shores remained unsettled. The interpretation of "right" and "liberty" proved a source of friction between the two nations. More importantly, Congress by the treaty was pledged to "earnestly recommend" to the legislatures of the states a full restoration of the rights and property of "real British subjects" as well as of Loyalists who had not borne arms against the United States, and further pledged that there would be no future confiscation. These pledges proved to be a pious hope. Lastly, the treaty provided that the creditors on either side should meet with no lawful impediment to the recovery of all bona fide debts of the full value in pound sterling. This clause was to be bitterly contested in states like Virginia, whose tobacco planters were heavily indebted to British and Scottish factors.*

4. The Articles of Confederation, March 1, 1781*

To all to whom these presents shall come, we the undersigned delegates of the states affixed to our names send greeting. WHEREAS the delegates of the United States of America in Congress assembled did on the fifteenth day of November in the

* J. D. Richardson (ed.), *Compilation of Messages and Papers of the Presidents, 1789–1897*, 10 vols. (Washington, D.C., 1896), I, 9 et seq.

year of our Lord one thousand seven hundred and seventy-seven, and in the second year of the independence of America, agree to certain articles of confederation and perpetual union between the states of New Hampshire, Massachusetts Bay, Rhode Island and Providence Plantations, Connecticut, New York, New Jersey, Pennsylvania, Delaware, Maryland, Virginia, North Carolina, South Carolina, and Georgia. . . .

ARTICLE 1

The style of this confederacy shall be "The United States of America."

ARTICLE 2

Each state retains its sovereignty, freedom, and independence, and every power, jurisdiction, and right, which is not by this confederation expressly delegated to the United States, in Congress assembled.

ARTICLE 3

The said states hereby severally enter into a firm league of friendship with each other for their common defense, the security of their liberties, and their mutual and general welfare, binding themselves to assist each other against all force offered to, or attacks made upon them, or any of them, on account of religion, sovereignty, trade, or any other pretense whatever.

ARTICLE 4

The better to secure and perpetuate mutual friendship and intercourse among the people of the different states in this union, the free inhabitants of each of these states—paupers, vagabonds, and fugitives from justice excepted—shall be entitled to all privileges and immunities of free citizens in the several states; and the people of each state shall have free ingress and regress to and from any other state, and shall enjoy therein all the privileges of trade and commerce, subject to the same duties, impositions, and restrictions as the inhabitants thereof respectively, provided that such restrictions shall not extend so far as to prevent the removal of property imported into any state, to any other state of which the owner is an inhabitant; provided also that no imposition, duties, or restriction shall be laid by any state on the property of the United States, or either of them.

If any person guilty of, or charged with treason, felony, or other high misdemeanor in any state shall flee from justice, and be found in any of the United States, he shall upon demand of the governor or executive power of the state from which he fled be delivered up and removed to the state having jurisdiction of his offense.

Full faith and credit shall be given in each of these states to the records, acts, and judicial proceedings of the courts and magistrates of every other state.

ARTICLE 5

For the more convenient management of the general interests of the United States, delegates shall be annually appointed in such manner as the legislature of each state shall direct, to meet in Congress on the first Monday in November, in every year, with a power reserved to each state to recall its delegates, or any of them, at any time within the year, and to send others in their stead for the remainder of the year.

No state shall be represented in Congress by less than two, nor by more than seven members; and no person shall be capable of being a delegate for more than three years in any term of six years; nor shall any person being a delegate, be capable of holding any office under the United States for which he, or another for his benefit, receives any salary, fees, or emolument of any kind.

Each state shall maintain its own delegates in a meeting of the states, and while they act as members of the committee of the states.

In determining questions in the United States in Congress assembled, each state shall have one vote.

Freedom of speech and debate in Congress shall not be impeached or questioned in any court, or place out of Congress, and the members of Congress shall be protected in their persons from arrests and imprisonments during the time of their going to and from, and attendance on Congress, except for treason, felony, or breach of the peace.

ARTICLE 6

No state without the consent of the United States in Congress assembled shall send any embassy to, or receive any embassy from, or enter into any conference, agreement, or alliance or treaty with any king, prince, or state; nor shall any person holding any office of profit or trust under the United States, or any of them, accept of any present, emolument, office, or title of any kind whatever from any king, prince, or foreign state; nor shall the United States in Congress assembled, or any of them, grant any title of nobility.

No two or more states shall enter into any treaty, confederation, or alliance whatever between them without the consent of the United States in Congress assembled, specifying accurately the purposes for which the same is to be entered into, and how long it shall continue.

No state shall lay any imposts or duties which may interfere with any stipulations in treaties entered into by the United States in Congress assembled, with any king, prince, or state, in pursuance of any treaties already proposed by Congress to the courts of France and Spain.

No vessels of war shall be kept up in time of peace by any state, except such number only as shall be deemed necessary by the United States in Congress assembled, for the defense of such state, or its trade; nor shall any body of forces be kept up by any state in time of peace, except such number only as in the judgment of the United States, in Congress assembled, shall be deemed requisite to garrison the forts necessary for the defense of such state; but every state shall always keep up a well-regulated and disciplined militia, sufficiently armed and accoutered, and shall provide and constantly have ready for use, in public stores, a due number of field pieces and tents, and a proper quantity of arms, ammunition, and camp equipage.

No state shall engage in any war without the consent of the United States in Congress assembled, unless such state be actually invaded by enemies, or shall have received certain advice of a resolution being formed by some nation of Indians to invade such state, and the danger is so imminent as not to admit of a delay till the United States in Congress assembled can be consulted: nor shall any state grant commissions to any ships or vessels of war, nor letters of marque or reprisal, except it be after a declaration of war by the United States in Congress assembled, and then only against the kingdom or state and the subjects thereof, against which war has been so declared, and under such regulations as shall be established by the United States in Congress assembled, unless such state be infested by pirates, in which case vessels of war may be fitted out for that occasion and kept so long as the danger shall continue, or until the United States in Congress assembled shall determine otherwise.

ARTICLE 7

When land forces are raised by any state for the common defense, all officers of or under the rank of colonel shall be appointed by the legislature of each state respectively by whom such forces shall be raised, or in such manner as such state shall direct, and all vacancies shall be filled up by the state which first made the appointment.

ARTICLE 8

All charges of war, and all other expenses that shall be incurred for the common defense or general welfare, and allowed by the United States in Congress assembled, shall be defrayed out of a common treasury, which shall be supplied by the several states in proportion to the value of all land within each state, granted to or surveyed for any person, as such land and the buildings and improvements thereon shall be estimated according to such mode as the United States in Congress assembled shall from time to time direct and appoint. The taxes for paying that proportion shall be laid and levied by the authority and direction of the legislatures of the several states within the time agreed upon by the United States in Congress assembled.

ARTICLE 9

The United States in Congress assembled shall have the sole and exclusive right and power of determining on peace and war, except in the cases mentioned in the sixth article—of sending and receiving ambassadors—[of] entering into treaties and alliances, provided that no treaty of commerce shall be made whereby the legislative power of the respective states shall be restrained from imposing such imposts and duties on foreigners, as their own people are subjected to, or from prohibiting the exportation or importation of any species of goods or commodities whatsoever —of establishing rules for deciding in all cases, what captures on land or water shall be legal, and in what manner prizes taken by land or naval forces in the service of the United States shall be divided or appropriated—of granting letters of marque and reprisal in times of peace—[of] appointing courts for the trial of piracies and felonies committed on the high seas and establishing courts for receiving and determining finally appeals in all cases of captures, provided that no member of Congress shall be appointed a judge of any of the said courts.

The United States in Congress assembled shall also be the last resort on appeal in all disputes and differences now subsisting or that hereafter may arise between two or more states concerning boundary, jurisdiction, or any other cause whatever; which authority shall always be exercised in the manner following:

Whenever the legislative or executive authority or lawful agent of any state in controversy with another shall present a petition to Congress, stating the matter in question and praying for a hearing, notice thereof shall be given by order of Congress to the legislative or executive authority of the other state in controversy, and a day assigned for the appearance of the parties by their lawful agents, who shall then be directed to appoint by joint consent, commissioners or judges to constitute a court for hearing and determining the matter in question: but if they cannot agree, Congress shall name three persons out of each of the United States, and from the list of such persons each party shall alternately strike out one, the petitioners beginning, until the number shall be reduced to thirteen; and from that number not less than seven nor more than nine names, as Congress shall direct, shall in the presence of Congress be drawn out by lot, and the persons whose names shall be so drawn, or any five of them, shall be commissioners or judges to hear and finally determine the controversy; so always as a major part of the judges who shall hear the cause shall agree in the determination: and if either party shall neglect to attend at the day appointed, without showing reasons, which Congress shall judge sufficient, or being present shall refuse to strike, the Congress shall proceed to nominate three persons out of each state, and the secretary of Congress shall strike in behalf of such party absent or refusing; and the judgment and sentence of the court to be appointed, in the manner before prescribed, shall be final and conclusive; and if any of the parties shall refuse to submit to the authority of such court, or to appear to defend their claim or cause, the court shall nevertheless proceed to pronounce sentence, or judgment, which shall in like manner be final and decisive, the judgment or sentence and other proceedings being in either case transmitted to Congress and lodged among the acts of Congress for the security of the parties concerned: provided that every commissioner, before he sits in judgment, shall take an oath to be administered by one of the judges of the supreme or superior court of the state where the cause shall be tried, "well and truly to hear and determine the matter in question, according to the best of his judgment, without favor, affection, or hope of reward": provided also that no state shall be deprived of territory for the benefit of the United States.

All controversies concerning the private right of soil claimed under different grants of two or more states, whose jurisdiction as they may respect such lands, and the states which passed such grants are adjusted, the said grants or either of them being at the same time claimed to have originated antecedent to such settlement of jurisdiction, shall on the petition of either party on the Congress of the United States, be finally determined as near as may be in the same manner as before prescribed for deciding disputes respecting territorial jurisdiction between different states.

The United States in Congress assembled shall also have the sole and exclusive right and power of regulating the alloy and value of coin struck by their own authority, or by that of the respective tests—fixing the standard of weights and measures throughout the United States—regulating the trade and managing all affairs with the Indians, not members of any of the states, provided that the legislative right of any state within its own limits be not infringed or violated—establishing and regulating post offices from one state to another throughout all the United States, and exacting such postage on the papers passing through the same as may be requisite to defray the expenses of the said office—appointing all officers of the land forces in the service of the United States, excepting regimental officers—appointing all the officers of the naval forces, and commissioning all officers whatever in the service of the United States—making rules for the government and regulation of the said land and naval forces, and directing their operations.

The United States in Congress assembled shall have authority to appoint a committee to sit in the recess of Congress, to be denominated a "Committee of the States," and to consist of one delegate from each state; and to appoint such other committees and civil officers as may be necessary for managing the general affairs of the United States under their direction—to appoint one of their number to preside, provided that no person be allowed to serve in the office of president more than one year in any term of three years; to ascertain the necessary sums of money to be raised for the service of the United States, and to appropriate and apply the same for defraying the public expenses—to borrow money or emit bills on the credit of the United States, transmitting every half-year to the respective states an account of the sums of money so borrowed or emitted—to build and equip a navy—to agree upon the number of land forces, and to make requisitions from each state for its quota in proportion to the number of white inhabitants in each state; which requisition shall be binding, and thereupon the legislature of each state shall appoint the regimental officers, raise the men, and clothe, arm, and equip them in a soldier-like manner at the expense of the United States, and the officers and men so clothed, armed, and equipped shall march to the place appointed, and within the time agreed on by the United States in Congress assembled: but if the United States in Congress assembled shall, on consideration of circumstances, judge proper that any state should not raise men, or should raise a smaller number of men than the quota thereof, and that any other state should raise a greater number of men than the quota thereof, such extra number shall be raised, officered, clothed, armed, and equipped in the same manner as the quota of such state unless the legislature of such state shall judge that such extra number cannot be safely spared out of the same, in which case they shall raise, officer, clothe, arm, and equip as many of such extra number as they judge can be safely spared. And the officers and men so clothed, armed, and equipped shall march to the place appointed, and within the time agreed on by the United States in Congress assembled.

The United States in Congress assembled shall never engage in a war, nor grant letters of marque and reprisal in time of peace, nor enter into any treaties or alliances, nor coin money, nor regulate the value thereof, nor ascertain the sums and expenses necessary for the defense and welfare of the United States, or any of them, nor emit bills, nor borrow money on the credit of the United States, nor appropriate money, nor agree upon the number of vessels of war to be built or purchased, nor the number of land or sea forces to be raised, nor appoint a commander-in-chief of the army or navy, unless nine states assent to the same: nor shall a question on any other point, except for adjourning from day to day, be determined unless by the votes of a majority of the United States in Congress assembled.

The Congress of the United States shall have power to adjourn to any time within the year, and to any place within the United States, so that no period of adjournment be for a longer duration than the space of six months, and shall publish the journal of their proceedings monthly, except such parts thereof relating to treaties, alliances, or military operations, as in their judgment require secrecy; and the yeas and nays of the delegates of each state on any question shall be entered on the journal when it is desired by any delegate; and the delegates of a state, or any of them, at his or their request shall be furnished with a transcript of the said journal, except such parts as are above excepted, to lay before the legislatures of the several states.

ARTICLE 10

The committee of the states, or any nine of them, shall be authorized to execute, in the recess of Congress, such of the powers of Congress as the United States in Congress assembled, by the consent of nine states, shall from time to time think expedient to vest them with; provided that no power be delegated to the said committee for the exercise of which, by the Articles of Confederation, the voice of nine states in the Congress of the United States assembled is requisite.

ARTICLE 11

Canada acceding to this confederation, and joining in the measures of the United States, shall be admitted into, and entitled to all the advantages of this union: but no other colony shall be admitted into the same unless such admission be agreed to by nine states.

ARTICLE 12

All bills of credit emitted, monies borrowed, and debts contracted by, or under the authority of Congress, before the assembling of the United States, in pursuance of the present confederation, shall be deemed and considered as a charge against the United States, for payment and satisfaction whereof the said United States and the public faith are hereby solemnly pledged.

ARTICLE 13

Every state shall abide by the determinations of the United States in Congress assembled on all questions which, by this confederation, are submitted to them. And the articles of this confederation shall be inviolably observed by every state, and the union shall be perpetual; nor shall any alteration at any time hereafter be made in any of them, unless such alteration be agreed to in a Congress of the United States, and be afterward confirmed by the legislatures of every state.

AND WHEREAS, It hath pleased the Great Governor of the World to incline the hearts of the legislatures we respectively represent in Congress to approve of, and to authorize us to ratify, the said Articles of Confederation and perpetual union: KNOW YE, That we the undersigned delegates, by virtue of the power and authority to us given for that purpose, do by these presents, in the name and in behalf of our respective constituents, fully and entirely ratify and confirm each and every of the said Articles of Confederation and perpetual union, and all and singular the matters and things therein contained: and we do further solemnly plight and engage the faith of our respective constituents, that they shall abide by the determinations of the United States in Congress assembled, on all questions which, by the said confederation, are submitted to them. And that the articles thereof shall be inviolably observed by the states we respectively represent, and that the union shall be perpetual. In witness whereof we have hereunto set our hands in Congress.

Done at Philadelphia in the State of Pennsylvania the ninth day of July in the year of our Lord one thousand seven hundred and seventy-eight, and in the third year of the independence of America.

5. The Definitive Treaty of Peace

*Signed at Paris, September 3, 1783 ***

In the Name of the most Holy & undivided Trinity.

It having pleased the divine Providence to dispose the Hearts of the most Serene and most Potent Prince George the third, by the Grace of God, King of Great Britain, France & Ireland, Defender of the Faith, Duke of Brunswick and Lunebourg, Arch Treasurer, and Prince Elector of the Holy Roman Empire &c[a] and of the United States of America, to forget all past Misunderstandings and Differences that have unhappily interrupted the good Correspondence and Friendship which they mutually wish to restore; and to establish such a beneficial and satisfactory Intercourse between the two Countries upon the Ground of reciprocal Advantages and mutual Convenience as may promote and secure to both perpetual Peace & Harmony, and having for this desirable End already laid the Foundation of Peace & Reconciliation by the Provisional Articles signed at Paris on the

* Richard B. Morris, *The Peacemakers* (New York, 1965), 461–465.

30th of Novr 1782. by the Commissioners empower'd on each Part, which Articles were agreed to be inserted in and to constitute the Treaty of Peace proposed to be concluded between the Crown of Great Britain and the said United States, but which Treaty was not to be concluded until Terms of Peace should be agreed upon between Great Britain & France, And his Britannic Majesty should be ready to conclude such Treaty accordingly: and the Treaty between Great Britain & France having since been concluded, His Britannic Majesty & the United States of America, in Order to carry into full Effect the Provisional Articles abovementioned, according to the Tenor thereof, have constituted & appointed, that is to say His Britannic Majesty on his Part, David Hartley Esqr, Member of the Parliament of Great Britain; and the said United States on their Part, John Adams Esqr, late a Commissioner of the United States of America at the Court of Versailles, late Delegate in Congress from the State of Massachusetts and Chief Justice of the said State, and Minister Plenipotentiary of the said United States to their High Mightinesses the States General of the United Netherlands; Benjamin Franklin Esqre late Delegate in Congress from the State of Pennsylvania, President of the Convention of the s^d State, and Minister Plenipotentiary from the United States of America at the Court of Versailles; John Jay Esqre late President of Congress, and Chief Justice of the State of New-York & Minister Plenipotentiary from the said United States at the Court of Madrid; to be the Plenipotentiaries for the concluding and signing the Present Definitive Treaty; who after having reciprocally communicated their respective full Powers have agreed upon and confirmed the following Articles.

ARTICLE 1st

His Britannic Majesty acknowledges the s^d United States, viz. New-Hampshire Massachusetts Bay, Rhode-Island & Providence Plantations, Connecticut, New York, New Jersey, Pennsylvania, Delaware, Maryland, Virginia, North Carolina, South Carolina & Georgia, to be free sovereign & Independent States; that he treats with them as such, and for himself his Heirs & Successors, relinquishes all Claims to the Government Propriety & Territorial Rights of the same & every Part thereof.

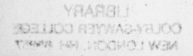

ARTICLE 2ᵈ

And that all Disputes which might arise in future on the Subject of the Boundaries of the said United States, may be prevented, it is hereby agreed and declared, that the following are and shall be their Boundaries, Viz. From the North West Angle of Nova Scotia, viz. That Angle which is formed by a Line drawn due North from the Source of Saint Croix River to the Highlands along the said Highlands which divide those Rivers that empty themselves into the River St Lawrence, from those which fall into the Atlantic Ocean, to the Northwestern-most Head of Connecticut River: Thence down along the middle of that River to the forty fifth Degree of North Latitude; From thence by a Line due West on said Latitude until it strikes the River Iroquois or Cataraquy; Thence along the middle of said River into Lake Ontario; through the Middle of said Lake until it strikes the Communication by Water between that Lake & Lake Erie; Thence along the middle of said Communication into Lake Erie; through the middle of said Lake, until it arrives at the Water Communication between that Lake & Lake Huron; Thence along the middle of said Water-Communication into the Lake Huron, thence through the middle of said Lake to the Water Communication between that Lake and Lake Superior, thence through Lake Superior Northward of the Isles Royal & Phelipeaux to the Long Lake; Thence through the Middle of said Long-Lake, and the Water Communication between it & the Lake of the Woods, to the said Lake of the Woods; Thence through the said Lake to the most Northwestern Point thereof, and from thence on a due West Course to the River Mississippi, Thence by a Line to be drawn along the Middle of the said River Mississippi until it shall intersect the Northernmost Part of the thirty first Degree of North Latitude. South, by a Line to be drawn due East from the Determination of the Line last mentioned, in the Latitude of thirty one Degrees North of the Equator to the middle of the River Apalachicola or Catahouche. Thence along the middle thereof to its Junction with the Flint River; Thence strait to the Head of St Mary's River, and thence down along the middle of St Mary's River to the Atlantic Ocean. East, by a Line to be drawn along the Middle of the River St Croix, from its Mouth

in the Bay of Fundy to its Source; and from its Source directly
North to the aforesaid Highlands, which divide the Rivers that
fall into the Atlantic Ocean, from those which fall into the River
St Lawrence; comprehending all Islands within twenty Leagues
of any Part of the Shores of the United States, & lying between
Lines to be drawn due East from the Points where the aforesaid
Boundaries between Nova Scotia on the one Part and East
Florida on the other, shall respectively touch the Bay of Fundy
and the Atlantic Ocean, excepting such Islands as now are or
heretofore have been within the Limits of the said Province of
Nova Scotia.

ARTICLE 3^d

It is agreed that the People of the United States shall continue to enjoy unmolested the Right to take Fish of every kind
on the Grand Bank and on all the other Banks of New-foundland, also in the Gulph of St Lawrence, and at all other Places
in the Sea where the Inhabitants of both Countries used at any
time heretofore to fish. And also that the Inhabitants of the
United States shall have Liberty to take Fish of every Kind on
such Part of the Coast of New-foundland as British Fishermen
shall use, (but not to dry or cure the same on that Island) And
also on the Coasts Bays & Creeks of all other of his Britannic
Majesty's Dominions in America, and that the American Fishermen shall have Liberty to dry and cure Fish in any of the
unsettled Bays Harbours and Creeks of Nova Scotia, Magdalen
Islands, and Labrador, so long as the same shall remain unsettled but so soon as the same or either of them shall be settled,
it shall not be lawful for the said Fishermen to dry or cure Fish
at such Settlement, without a previous Agreement for that purpose with the Inhabitants, Proprietors or Possessors of the
Ground.

ARTICLE 4th

It is agreed that Creditors on either Side shall meet with no
lawful Impediment to the Recovery of the full Value in Sterling
Money of all bona fide Debts heretofore contracted.

ARTICLE 5th

It is agreed that the Congress shall earnestly recommend it to the Legislatures of the respective States to provide for the Restitution of all Estates, Rights and Properties which have been confiscated belonging to real British Subjects; and also of the Estates Rights and Properties of Persons resident in Districts in the Possession of his Majesty's Arms, and who have not borne Arms against the said United States. And that Persons of any other Description shall have free Liberty to go to any Part or Parts of any of the thirteen United States and therein to remain twelve Months unmolested in their Endeavours to obtain the Restitution of such of their Estates Rights & Properties as may have been confiscated. And that Congress shall also earnestly recommend to the several States, a Reconsideration and Revision of all Acts or Laws regarding the Premises, so as to render the said Laws or Acts perfectly consistent, not only with Justice and Equity, but with that Spirit of Conciliation, which, on the Return of the Blessings of Peace should universally prevail. And that Congress shall also earnestly recommend to the several States, that the Estates, Rights and Properties of such last mentioned Persons shall be restored to them, they refunding to any Persons who may be now in Possession, the Bonâ fide Price (where any has been given) which such Persons may have paid on purchasing any of the said Lands, Rights or Properties, since the Confiscation.

And it is agreed that all Persons who have any Interest in confiscated Lands, either by Debts, Marriage Settlements, or otherwise, shall meet with no lawful Impediment in the Prosecution of their just Rights.

ARTICLE 6th

That there shall be no future Confiscations made nor any Prosecutions commenc'd against any Person or Persons for or by Reason of the Part, which he or they may have taken in the present War, and that no Person shall on that Account suffer any future Loss or Damage, either in his Person Liberty or Property; and that those who may be in Confinement on such Charges at the Time of the Ratification of the Treaty in America shall be immediately set at Liberty, and the Prosecutions so commenced be discontinued.

ARTICLE 7th

There shall be a firm and perpetual Peace between his Britannic Majesty and the said States and between the Subjects of the one, and the Citizens of the other, wherefore all Hostilities both by Sea and Land shall from henceforth cease: All Prisoners on both Sides shall be set at Liberty, and his Britannic Majesty shall with all convenient speed, and without causing any Destruction, or carrying away any Negroes or other Property of the American Inhabitants, withdraw all his Armies, Garrisons & Fleets from the said United States, and from every Port, Place and Harbour within the same; leaving in all Fortifications the American Artillery that may be therein: And shall also Order & cause all Archives, Records, Deeds & Papers belonging to any of the said States, or their Citizens, which in the Course of the War may have fallen into the Hands of his Officers, to be forthwith restored and deliver'd to the proper States and Persons to whom they belong.

ARTICLE 8th

The Navigation of the River Mississippi, from its source to the Ocean shall for ever remain free and open to the Subjects of Great Britain and the Citizens of the United States.

ARTICLE 9th

In Case it should so happen that any Place or Territory belonging to great Britain or to the United States should have been conquer'd by the Arms of either from the other before the Arrival of the said Provisional Articles in America it is agreed that the same shall be restored without Difficulty and without requiring any Compensation.

ARTICLE 10th

The solemn Ratifications of the present Treaty expedited in good & due Form shall be exchanged between the contracting Parties in the Space of Six Months or sooner if possible to be computed from the Day of the Signature of the present Treaty. In Witness whereof we the undersigned their Ministers Plenipotentiary have in their Name and in Virtue of our Full Powers signed with our Hands the present Definitive Treaty, and caused the Seals of our Arms to be affix'd thereto.

Done at Paris, this third Day of September, In the Year of our Lord one thousand seven hundred & eighty three.

D HARTLEY   JOHN ADAMS   B FRANKLIN   JOHN JAY
[Seal]   [Seal]   [Seal]   [Seal]

Chapter III

THE PROBLEM OF THE PUBLIC CREDITORS AND THE ARMY

Taking over as Superintendent of Finance at a time of national insolvency, Robert Morris imposed rigid economies in order to achieve a balanced budget. To maintain the solvency of his own administration, he refused to pay claims, including interest on the public debt originating before January 1, 1782, the date he entered upon his office. In addition, the soldiers and officers received virtually nothing in 1781 and 1782. The public creditors and the army now became a common interest group determined to see that an effective government was instituted capable of meeting its obligations.

Beset by its inability to secure the adoption by the states of an impost, Congress turned down the plea of the officers for a life pension at half pay or six years at full pay. Resenting the shabby treatment at the hands of their government, a number of officers at army headquarters at Newburgh, supported by General Horatio Gates and several nationalist-minded civilian leaders, circulated an address written by Major John Armstrong. A month earlier Hamilton, in an indiscreet letter to General Washington, urged the army's case and suggested not only that the military might force a showdown over the issue but that the General himself, rather than discountenance such efforts, take over the direction of them.

If Hamilton voiced the views of the public creditors and some officers, he was quickly disabused. Washington could not fail to heed the implied threat of a military coup contained in Hamilton's letter and in the Newburgh Address with its castigation of Congress for its treatment of the soldiers.

At the strategic moment Washington asserted his leadership to prevent a show of force. The plotters had called for a meeting on March 15th to draft a "last remonstrance" or ultimatum. To their consternation Washington appeared, and while he promised quick redress for the soldiers' grievances, he denounced the resort to immoderate measures. The effect of his appearance and remarks was electric. The officers declared their "unshaken confidence in the justice of Congress" and repudiated the Newburgh Address. A week later Congress, upon Washington's insistence, approved an act granting the officers a sum equal to five years' full pay.

The thwarting of the Newburgh plot did not allay suspicions on the part of many citizens of the influence of the army. These suspicions were quickened by the formation of the Order of the Cincinnati. Ostensibly a veterans organization created to perpetuate the memory of the heroic struggle against Britain and to aid the widows and orphans of former soldiers, the Society was widely criticized for adopting the principle of hereditary membership. It was feared in some quarters that the Order might use its weight to form an hereditary aristocracy in America and establish a strongly centralized state. The most extreme criticism of the Cincinnati came from the pen of Aedanus Burke, a South Carolina judge, whose pamphlet concerning the dangers of the Cincinnati attained wide circulation and numerous reprintings. In France, Mirabeau, soon to be a revolutionary protagonist in his own land, issued his own adaptation and amplification of Burke's indictment. Bowing to the international clamor, the Order of the Cincinnati promptly abolished its hereditary character and placed the funds of the state societies in the keeping of the state legislatures.

6. Reaction to Military Conspirators: The Newburgh Address, March 11, 1783*

To the Officers of the Army.

Gentlemen,—A fellow soldier, whose interest and affections bind him strongly to you, whose past sufferings have been as great, and whose future fortune may be as desperate as yours— would beg leave to address you.

Age has its claims, and rank is not without its pretensions to advise: but, though unsupported by both, he flatters himself, that the plain language of sincerity and experience will neither be unheard nor unregarded.

Like many of you, he loved private life, and left it with regret. He left it, determined to retire from the field, with the necessity that called him to it, and not till then—not till the enemies of his country, the slaves of power, and the hirelings of injustice, were compelled to abandon their schemes, and acknowledge America as terrible in arms as she had been humble in remonstrance. With this object in view, he has long shared in your toils and mingled in your dangers. He has felt the cold hand of poverty without a murmur, and has seen the insolence of wealth without a sigh. But, too much under the direction of his wishes, and sometimes weak enough to mistake desire for opinion, he has till lately—very lately—believed in the justice of his country. He hoped that, as the clouds of adversity scattered, and as the sunshine of peace and better fortune broke in upon us, the coldness and severity of government would relax, and that, more than

* W. C. Ford, *et al.* (eds.), *Journals of the Continental Congress,* 34 vols. (Washington, D.C., 1904–37), XXIV, 295–297.

justice, that gratitude would blaze forth upon those hands, which had upheld her, in the darkest stages of her passage, from impending servitude to acknowledged independence. But faith has its limits as well as temper, and there are points beyond which neither can be stretched, without sinking into cowardice or plunging into credulity.—This, my friends, I conceive to be your situation.—Hurried to the very verge of both, another step would ruin you forever.—To be tame and unprovoked when injuries press hard upon you, is more than weakness; but to look up for kinder usage, without one manly effort of your own, would fix your character, and shew the world how richly you deserve those chains you broke. To guard against this evil, let us take a review of the ground upon which we now stand, and from thence carry our thoughts forward for a moment, into the unexplored field of expedient.

After a pursuit of seven long years, the object for which we set out is at length brought within our reach. Yes, my friends, that suffering courage of yours was active once—it has conducted the United States of America through a doubtful and a bloody war. It has placed her in the chair of independency, and peace returns again to bless—whom? A country willing to redress your wrongs, cherish your worth and reward your services, a country courting your return to private life, with tears of gratitude and smiles of admiration, longing to divide with you that independency which your gallantry has given, and those riches which your wounds have preserved? Is this the case? Or is it rather a country that tramples upon your rights, disdains your cries and insults your distresses? Have you not, more than once, suggested your wishes, and made known your wants to Congress? Wants and wishes which gratitude and policy should have anticipated, rather than evaded. And have you not lately, in the meek language of entreating memorials, begged from their justice, what you would no longer expect from their favour? How have you been answered? Let the letter which you are called to consider to-morrow make reply.

If this, then, be your treatment, while the swords you wear are necessary for the defence of America, what have you to expect from peace, when your voice shall sink, and your strength dissipate by division? When those very swords, the instruments and companions of your glory, shall be taken from your sides, and no remaining mark of military distinction left but your wants, infirmities and scars? Can you then consent to be the only sufferers by this revolution, and retiring from the field, grow old in poverty, wretchedness and contempt? Can you consent to wade through the vile mire of dependency, and owe the miserable remnant of that life to charity, which has hitherto been spent in honor? If you can—GO—and carry with you the jest of tories and scorn of whigs—the ridicule, and what is worse, the pity of the world. Go, starve, and be forgotten! But, if your spirit should revolt at this; if you have sense enough to discover, and spirit enough to oppose tyranny under whatever garb it may assume; whether it be the plain coat of republicanism, or the splendid robe of royalty; if you have yet learned to discriminate between a people and a cause, between men and principles—awake; attend to your situation and redress yourselves. If the present moment be lost, every future effort is in vain; and your threats then, will be as empty as your entreaties now.

I would advise you, therefore, to come to some final opinion upon what you can bear, and what you will suffer. If your determination be in any proportion to your wrongs, carry your appeal from the justice to the fears of government. Change the milk-and-water style of your last memorial; assume a bolder tone—decent, but lively, spirited and determined, and suspect the man who would advise to more moderation and longer forbearance. Let two or three men, who can feel as well as write, be appointed to draw up your last remonstrance; for, I would no longer give it the sueing, soft, unsuccessful epithet of memorial. Let it be represented in language that will neither dishonor you by its rudeness, nor betray you by its fears, what has been promised by Congress, and what has been performed, how long and how patiently you have suffered, how little you have asked, and how much of that little has been denied. Tell them that, though you were the first, and would wish to be the last to encounter danger: though despair itself can never drive you into dishonor, it may drive you from the field: that the wound often irritated, and never healed, may at length become incurable; and that the slightest mark of indignity from Congress now, must operate like the grave, and part you forever: that in any political event, the army has its alternative. If peace, that nothing shall separate them from your arms but death: if war, that courting the auspices, and inviting the direction of your illustrious leader, you will retire to some unsettled country, smile in your turn, and "mock when their fear cometh on." But let it represent also, that should they comply with the request of your late memorial, it would make you more happy and them more respectable. That while war should continue, you would follow their standard into the field, and when it came to an end, you would withdraw into the shade of private life, and give the world another subject of wonder and applause; an army victorious over its enemies—victorious over itself.

7. Army Coup Subdued: George Washington's Appeal to the Officers of the Army, March 15, 1783 *

Head Quarters, Newburgh
March 15, 1783.

To The Officers of the Army

Gentlemen: By an anonymous summons, an attempt has been made to convene you together; how inconsistent with the rules of propriety! how unmilitary! and how subversive of all order and discipline, let the good sense of the Army decide.

In the moment of this Summons, another anonymous production was sent into circulation, addressed more to the feelings and passions, than to the reason and judgment of the Army. The author of the piece, is entitled to much credit for the goodness

* J. C. Fitzpatrick, *Writings of George Washington*, 39 vols. (Washington, 1931–44), XXVI, 222–227.

of his Pen and I could wish he had as much credit for the rectitude of his Heart, for, as Men see thro' different Optics, and are induced by the reflecting faculties of the Mind, to use different means, to attain the same end, the Author of the Address, should have had more charity, than to mark for Suspicion, the Man who should recommend moderation and longer forbearance, or, in other words, who should not think as he thinks, and act as he advises. But he had another plan in view, in which candor and liberality of Sentiment, regard to justice, and love of Country, have no part; and he was right, to insinuate the darkest suspicion, to effect the blackest designs.

That the Address is drawn with great Art, and is designed to answer the most insidious purposes. That it is calculated to impress the Mind, with an idea of premeditated injustice in the Sovereign power of the United States, and rouse all those resentments which must unavoidably flow from such a belief. That the secret mover of this Scheme (whoever he may be) intended to take advantage of the passions, while they were warmed by the recollection of past distresses, without giving time for cool, deliberative thinking, and that composure of Mind which is so necessary to give dignity and stability to measures is rendered too obvious, by the mode of conducting the business, to need other proof than a reference to the proceeding.

Thus much, Gentlemen, I have thought it incumbent on me to observe to you, to shew upon what principles I opposed the irregular and hasty meeting which was proposed to have been held on Tuesday last: and not because I wanted a disposition to give you every opportunity consistent with your own honor, and the dignity of the Army, to make known your grievances. If my conduct heretofore, has not evinced to you, that I have been a faithful friend to the Army, my declaration of it at this time wd. be equally unavailing and improper. But as I was among the first who embarked in the cause of our common Country. As I have never left your side one moment, but when called from you on public duty. As I have been the constant companion and witness of your Distresses, and not among the last to feel, and acknowledge your Merits. As I have ever considered my own Military reputation as inseperably connected with that of the Army. As my Heart has ever expanded with joy, when I have heard its praises, and my indignation has arisen, when the mouth of detraction has been opened against it, it can *scarcely be supposed,* at this late stage of the War, that I am indifferent to its interests. But, how are they to be promoted? The way is plain, says the anonymous Addresser. If War continues, remove into the unsettled Country; there establish yourselves, and leave an ungrateful Country to defend itself. But who are they to defend? Our Wives, our Children, our Farms, and other property which we leave behind us, or, in this state of hostile seperation, are we to take the two first (the latter cannot be removed), to perish in a Wilderness, with hunger, cold and nakedness? If Peace takes place, never sheath your Swords Says he untill you have obtained full and ample justice; this dreadful alternative, of either deserting our Country in the extremest hour of her distress, or turning our Arms against it, (which is the apparent object, unless Congress can be compelled into instant compliance) has something so shocking in it, that humanity revolts at the idea. My God! what can this writer have in view, by recommending such measures? Can he be a friend to the Army? Can he be a friend to this Country? Rather, is he not an insidious Foe? Some Emissary, perhaps, from New York, plotting the ruin of both, by sowing the seeds of discord and seperation between the Civil and Military powers of the Continent? And what a Compliment does he pay to our Understandings, when he recommends measures in either alternative, impracticable in their Nature?

But here, Gentlemen, I will drop the curtain, because it wd. be as imprudent in me to assign my reasons for this opinion, as it would be insulting to your conception, to suppose you stood in need of them. A moment's reflection will convince every dispassionate Mind of the physical impossibility of carrying either proposal into execution.

There might, Gentlemen, be an impropriety in my taking notice, in this Address to you, of an anonymous production, but the manner in which that performance has been introduced to the Army, the effect it was intended to have, together with some other circumstances, will amply justify my observations on the tendency of that Writing. With respect to the advice given by the Author, to suspect the Man, who shall recommend moderate measures and longer forbearance, I spurn it, as every Man, who regards that liberty, and reveres that justice for which we contend, undoubtedly must; for if Men are to be precluded from offering their Sentiments on a matter, which may involve the most serious and alarming consequences, that can invite the consideration of Mankind, reason is of no use to us; the freedom of Speech may be taken away, and, dumb and silent we may be led, like sheep, to the Slaughter.

I cannot, in justice to my own belief, and what I have great reason to conceive is the intention of Congress, conclude this Address, without giving it as my decided opinion, that that Honble Body, entertain exalted sentiments of the Services of the Army; and, from a full conviction of its merits and sufferings, will do it compleat justice. That their endeavors, to discover and establish funds for this purpose, have been unwearied, and will not cease, till they have succeeded, I have not a doubt. But, like all other large Bodies, where there is a variety of different Interests to reconcile, their deliberations are slow. Why then should we distrust them? and, in consequence of that distrust, adopt measures, which may cast a shade over that glory which, has been so justly acquired; and tarnish the reputation of an Army which is celebrated thro' all Europe, for its fortitude and Patriotism? and for what is this done? to bring the object we seek nearer? No! most certainly, in my opinion, it will cast it at a greater distance.

For myself (and I take no merit in giving the assurance, being induced to it from principles of gratitude, veracity and justice), a grateful sence of the confidence you have ever placed in me, a recollection of the chearful assistance, and prompt obedience I have experienced from you, under every vicissitude of Fortune, and the sincere affection I feel for an Army, I have so long had the honor to Command, will oblige me to declare, in this public and solemn manner, that, in the attainment of compleat justice for all your toils and dangers, and in the gratification of every wish, so far as may be done consistently with the great duty I owe my Country, and those powers we are bound to respect, you may freely command my Services to the utmost of my abilities.

While I give you these assurances, and pledge myself in the

most unequivocal manner, to exert whatever ability I am possessed of, in your favor, let me entreat you, Gentlemen, on your part, not to take any measures, which, viewed in the calm light of reason, will lessen the dignity, and sully the glory you have hitherto maintained; let me request you to rely on the plighted faith of your Country, and place a full confidence in the purity of the intentions of Congress; that, previous to your dissolution as an Army they will cause all your Accts. to be fairly liquidated, as directed in their resolutions, which were published to you two days ago, and that they will adopt the most effectual measures in their power, to render ample justice to you, for your faithful and meritorious Services. And let me conjure you, in the name of our common Country, as you value your own sacred honor, as you respect the rights of humanity, and as you regard the Military and National character of America, to express your utmost horror and detestation of the Man who wishes, under any specious pretences, to overturn the liberties of our Country, and who wickedly attempts to open the flood Gates of Civil discord, and deluge our rising Empire in Blood. By thus determining, and thus acting, you will pursue the plain and direct road to the attainment of your wishes. You will defeat the insidious designs of our Enemies, who are compelled to resort from open force to secret Artifice. You will give one more distinguished proof of unexampled patriotism and patient virtue, rising superior to the pressure of the most complicated sufferings; And you will, by the dignity of your Conduct, afford occasion for Posterity to say, when speaking of the glorious example you have exhibited to Mankind, "had this day been wanting, the World had never seen the last stage of perfection to which human nature is capable of attaining."

8.   A Warning Against Establishment of a Military Caste: Aedanus Burke's *Considerations on the Society or Order of Cincinnati*, 1783 *

The following publication is intended to convey a few observations to my fellow citizens, on a new *Society or Institution* lately established throughout the continent, composed of the Major-Generals, Brigadiers, and other Officers of our army. It is instituted by the name of "THE SOCIETY OF THE CIN-CINNATI" and it has arrived to considerable strength and maturity already. For besides the Grand or *General Society* of this order, a subordinate or *State Society* is established in each state and these again subdivided "into such districts as shall be directed by the State Societies. The General Society is to be held on the first Monday in May annually, so long as they shall deem necessary; and afterwards at least once in every three years. The state Societies are to meet the fourth of July annually, or oftener, if they shall find it expedient."

. . . It seems to be the offspring of patriotism, friendship, and humanity. And that many of the officers who have not closely viewed the subject, favour it from those principles, I have no doubt. But as several of them are equal in knowledge and abilities to any men in America, it is hardly possible but that some of them must feel into the nature and consequences of the institution. For to come to the second part of my argument, it is in reality, and will turn out to be, *an hereditary peerage;* a nobility to them and their *male issue,* and in default thereof, to the *collateral branches:* what the lawyers would call—A title of

* Aedanus Burke, *Considerations on the Society or Order of Cincinnati* (Philadelphia, 1783).

peerage of Cincinnati to them and their heirs male, remainder to their heirs general.

The sixth article of our confederation says, "Nor shall the United States in Congress assembled, nor any of them grant any title of nobility." But the order of Cincinnati usurp a nobility without gift or grant, in defiance of Congress and the states, as I shall shew presently. And though the order cannot, at present be sanctified by legal authority, yet that makes nothing against the consequences which will ensue. Though the Order is self-created, and an infringement of a general law of the Union; yet if the courage of the officers does not fail them; if they but keep up with firmness and perseverance against opposition, for this will be but trifling, so unthinking are the people; if they have but patience, subtilty, and address to cloke their design under a pious name of raising a charitable fund; so as to make it go down only for a few years; even if they are obliged from policy to lay aside the *badge and blue ribbon:* My life for it, they will have leisure to laugh at, and master their opponents. And the next generation will drink as deep of noble blood, and a hereditary peerage be as firmly settled in each potent family, and rivetted in our government, as any order of nobility is in the monarchies of Europe. This Order is planted in a fiery, hot ambition, and thirst for power; and its branches will end in tyranny. The Cincinnati will soon be corrupted, and the spirit of the people depressed; for in less than a century it will occasion such as inequality in the condition of our inhabitants, that the country will be composed only of two ranks of men: the patricians or nobles, and the rabble. This is the natural result of an establishment, whose departure is so sudden from our open professions of republicanism, that it must give a thinking mind most melancholy forebodings. This creating of a nobility, and breaking through our constitution; just as we were setting out in the world, is making that liberty which the Almighty has given us, a means for feeding our pride; and turning the blessings of Providence into a curse upon us.

Had this order been created by Congress or our own legislature, even in violation of the confederation and of our laws, I should not think it a matter of such moment: dukes, earls, or peers of the Cincinnati, sanctified by an act of Assembly or of

Congress, would be understood by all of us. Their pretensions and exclusive privileges, the mode of their trial for life and death, &c. ascertained. But the self-created Cincinnati, like a proud imperious man, would set no bounds to its claims. Jealous that it held not any thing on its own ambitious terms, as they had cut and carved titles for themselves and their posterity, they would be full grasping for every thing; and rising from one usurpation to another, as they succeeded. . . .

I mention these few plain notorious facts, to prove, that the institution of this nobility is not the way to promote and cherish *Union* and *National Honour.* Out of it will arise *discord* and not *union.* And that the people should, without so much as saying a word about the matter, behold this poisonous *exotic* plant taking root throughout the land. That they should commit such a vile abuse of their liberty as to allow it, is a reproach upon human nature; and would, in the eyes of posterity, be a national dishonour to us. I have often thought that the revolution in America would reduce it to a certainty, whether mankind was destined by nature for liberty or slavery; for a republican government never before has had, what we call fair play, in any part of the globe. But the Order of Cincinnati would give a fatal wound to civil liberty thro' the world, and prove to all that Plato, Sidney, Locke and others have bequeathed to posterity on the subject of political happiness, though appearing well on paper, yet was no more than ideal pictures of a fine imagination. Our example too would serve to strengthen tyranny in Europe, by evincing that a people brought up under a monarchy, and accustomed to be governed by others, are too degenerate to govern themselves in a state of liberty; and that after all we have done, we still keep a hankering after the orders, titles and trumpery we have been used to under the royal government, where the people are so bewitched, that abilities, virtue or wealth itself, are not such objects of reverence as a star or ribbon. . . .

I know it will be denied, that the Order is, what I do boldly assert it to be, an *hereditary peerage.* Some of its members assume the cloak of political modesty, and under it talk, that they are no more dangerous than a city corporation of "shopkeepers, taylors, or other mechanics; or like the Free Masons and other clubs who wear badges or medals." Here we see how ambition can assume all shapes and colours, and humble itself to the very dust to accomplish its purpose! This moment take upon them the superintendence of empire, the *honour, union and happiness of nations,* and the *exalted rights of human nature;* and the very next, prostrate themselves to the level of men, with whom to be compared on any other occasion, the Order would deem an insult. I say, that a body of military commanders, distinguished from the rest of society under an institution founded on the illustrious actions of so singular a revolution as that of America: invested with the exclusive privilege of wearing a badge of their order, honourable to themselves, as it is ignominious to the people; elevated above others, and in parity among themselves: These, I say, are peers of the realm, *pares regni,* and nothing more or less. And that this order being entailed on the *male issue,* and in default thereof, on the *collateral line,* makes it *hereditary.* And whether it be instituted by the legislature, who alone have the legal power to do it, or be usurped by the officers, it makes no difference in its consequences. For as I observed before, in one generation the order of Cincinnati will be established immoveably. The rank, number and influence of the members; the remembrance of their glorious actions, still heightened by the propensity of mankind to the marvellous: all this, I say, will raise the order to grandeur, antiquity, veneration and arbitrary power; acquisitions which will become hereditary with the peerage, and once obtained, not one family of them will ever think of renouncing.

Chapter IV

BRITISH DEBTS AND THE LOYALISTS

The peace treaty of 1783 stipulated that all private debts between Britons and Americans were still binding. This article incurred the wrath of many American debtors, especially planters in Virginia and Maryland. Both states had previously passed laws preventing British merchants from recovering prewar debts in the state courts. Although responsible men like George Mason, as his letter to Patrick Henry reveals, opposed any interference with the just collection of debts, other prominent Virginians, including Henry himself, were adamant and saw to it that state legislation and judicial decision hampered creditors at every turn. This noncompliance gave the British a ground for not relinquishing their military outposts on the northern and northwest frontiers.

Upon the conclusion of the war a number of persons who had remained neutral or had supported the British cause began returning to their homes and reclaiming their property. Militant Whigs were strongly opposed to permitting Loyalists, especially the wealthier, from resuming their prominent places in the community. Vindictive attacks upon Tories were now launched in the press, and those venturing to return to their homes were often threatened with physical violence. The article in the New York Packet is a fair sample of this anti-Tory line.

More serious than the vitriolic treatment of the Loyalists in the press was the enactment of legislation imperiling the civil rights of former Tories. For example, the New York state legislature passed a series of statutes destructive of the civil and political rights of the Loyalists and in derogation of the sixth article of the Treaty of Peace. Among these was the notorious Trespass Act of March 17, 1783, enabling those who had fled from the enemy to sue for trespass to their real or personal property during their absence, depriving defendants of the right to plead in justification any military order or command of the enemy for the occupation or destruction of the property. In Rutgers v. Waddington, the most notable case contested under this act, Alexander Hamilton took the unpopular cause of the defendant Loyalist Waddington. Hamilton argued that under international law the property was at the disposal of the occupation forces and that, in any event, an amnesty had been granted by the Treaty of Peace. The decision of the New York Mayor's Court, which heard the case, denied damages to the plaintiff for the period, 1780–83, when the defendant had occupied the property under license from the British commander-in-chief, in effect annulling the statute and anticipating judicial review. Extremists among the Patriots censured the court but Hamilton rushed into print with a defense of the decision in his vigorous Phocion letters. Supporting Hamilton, George Washington expressed his "hearty assent" to the judgment of the court. Ultimately the influence of the moderates brought about a modification of anti-Tory legislation.

Tories were no more scrupulous than Whigs in the methods they employed to reestablish their position in society. For example, Miers Fisher, a Quaker lawyer and former Tory exile, sought to obtain a charter for the Bank of Pennsylvania, a potential competitor of Robert Morris' Bank of North America. Among his arguments was the contention that the chartering of his bank would reduce the rate of interest, thus protecting the people against the exactions of the Jewish brokers. Not only was this a diversionary maneuver by which Tories attempted to exonerate themselves by inciting prejudice against Jews, but it was an implied attack on Robert Morris and his Bank, which had received support from Jews. The Philadelphia Independent Gazetteer printed a reply of one of the Jews whom Fisher had denounced. It is likely that the "Jew Broker" was none other than the patriot Haym Salomon.

9. Payment of Prewar Debts to British Merchants: George Mason to Patrick Henry, May 6, 1783*

The people in this part of the country are made very uneasy by the reports we have from below, that the Assembly will make some laws or resolutions, respecting British Debts, which may infringe the articles of the peace, under the mistaken idea, that Great Britain will not risque a renewal of the war on account of such an infraction of the treaty. We see by the late public papers, that the terms of the peace with America are so strongly censured in both Houses of parliament, that it has occasioned, or will occasion, a total change in the ministry. A new ministry averse to the treaty, or even the ministry who concluded it, might resent and revenge an infringement of it in any particular state, by reprisals upon the ships or coasts of such state, or by sending two or three Frigates to intercept their trade, without danger of involving themselves in a new war; for the power of war and peace, and of making treaties, being in Congress, and not in the separate states, any such act would be considered as an unwarrantable assumption of power in the state adopting it; and we have no reason to expect that either the late belligerent powers in Europe, or even the American states in general, would make a common cause of it. It is easy to foresee that in such an event our situation would neither be safe, or honorable.

Had it been in the power of the American commissioners (which it certainly was not) to have abolished the British debts here, it would have been but short sighted policy to have done so.

* W. W. Henry (ed.), *Patrick Henry*, 3 vols. (New York, 1891), II, 186–188.

The far fetch'd arguments which have been used to show the distinction between this and other wars, would not have been approved, or comprehended by the bulk of Mankind; and with what degree of confidence cou'd foreign merchants have ventured their effects here, if upon any national Quarrel, they were liable to confiscation? I could have wished indeed that some reasonable time had been allowed for the payment of British debts, and that the interest on them had been relinquished. As to the first, the desire of the British merchants to reinstate themselves in their trade here will probably prevent their pressing their debtors; and as to the last, their bond Debts only will carry interest. It is notorious that the custom of giving interest upon common accounts was introduced by the partiality of the merchants, of whom the jurys at the general court were chiefly composed for several years before the late revolution. Under our present circumstances, I think the accounts of British creditors may be safely trusted to the Virginia jurys, without any interposition of the Legislature.

In conversation upon this subject we sometimes hear a very absurd question: 'If we are now to pay the debts due the British merchants, what have we been fighting for all this while?' Surely not to avoid our just debts, or cheat our creditors; but to rescue our country from the oppression & tyranny of the British Government, and to secure the rights and liberty of ourselves, and our posterity; which we have happily accomplished. The ministry in Great Britain, and the torys here, have indeed constantly accused us of engaging in the war to avoid the payment of our debts; but every honest man has denied so injurious a charge with indignation. Upon the whole, we have certainly obtained better terms of peace than America had cause to expect; all the great points are ceded to us; and I cannot but think it would be highly dangerous and imprudent to risque a Breach of it.

The people here too, are greatly alarmed at a prevailing notion that those men who have paid British debts into the treasury in depreciated paper money, instead of making up the real value to their creditors, will now attempt to throw the difference upon the shoulders of the public, and levy it by taxes upon the people.

I should hope that such an iniquitous scheme will be rejected, with the contempt it deserves. If it is adopted, it will probably cause some violent convulsion; the people being determined, in many parts of the country, to form associations against it, and resist the payment of any taxes imposed on them for discharging the private debts of individuals.

10.   Anti-Tory Sentiment: "Probus" to the Whigs of New Jersey, April 17, 1783 *

To the Whigs of New Jersey

Independence and peace, which have been the objects of eight years severe contest, the ardent and constant desire of every American breast, are at length arrived; and each heart ought to glow with gratitude to the Divine Ruler of the universe for so great a blessing; but like all sublunary enjoyment, even these, the summit of our wishes, have come with their alloy. The article of giving the renegadoes, or tories, a temporary residence among us, is a bitter ingredient in this cup of happiness; and I am confident, from the known character of our worthy Commissioners, they never would have consented to it, had there been any mode to have avoided it, but by a continuation of the calamities of war; and even this, I doubt not, would have been preferred by those gentlemen, had they not put an entire confidence in your spirit, virtue and patriotism, believing that these would prevent what they could not.

Do not your spirits rise with indignation, your very blood curdle in your veins, at the idea of those Wretches, whose hands are still smoking with the blood of your slaughtered countrymen, brothers and fathers returning to live among you?—Are not the flames of your houses and temples always present before your

* *New York Packet,* April 17, 1783.

eyes, whenever you cast a thought on any of those minions?—
Can you detach the idea of a robber, an incendiary, or a mur-
derer, from one of their names?—If there are any among them
of the least spark of proper spirit, they will disdain the thought
of becoming humble suppliants to those whom they have so
much insulted and injured;—therefore none but those who are
entirely devoid of every genuine principle; viz. the abandoned
and profligate will return to us.—No method is left us to prevent
this calamity, but general associations to render their situation,
by every means in our power, so uneasy, that they will prefer a
voluntary banishment, to the proposed return. Let it be a crime
abhorrent to nature to have the least communication or intercourse with them. Like Cain of old, they will carry their mark in
their foreheads: Let them be avoided as persons contaminated
with the most deadly contagion, and remain as their just de-
merits "vagabonds upon the face of the earth." If this is not
done at first, and with spirit, time, and a continued intercourse,
will gradually lessen that detestation which every honest mind
must feel against them. The very money that they have gathered
from their treasons, their robberies, and murders, will enable
them to make some friends, and prepare the way for their final
flay. It is in your power, by the mode hinted at, to prevent these
evils. I beseech, I implore, I obtest you, by the means of your
slaughtered friends! By the cries of your deflowered virgins! And
abused matrons! By the flames of your houses! Your temples!
And your villages! By the calamities you have endured in a seven
years war! That you forget all animosities among yourselves, and
associate, and combine as one man to deprecate, and by proper
measures, to prevent miseries more direful than even war itself.

PROBUS

11. Defense of Loyalists: Alexander Hamilton's "Phocion" Letter, 1784 *

The persons alluded to pretend to appeal to the spirit of Whiggism; while they endeavor to put in motion all the furious and dark passions of the human mind. The spirit of Whiggism is generous, humane, beneficent, and just. These men inculcate revenge, cruelty, persecution and perfidy. The spirit of Whiggism cherishes legal liberty, holds the rights of every individual sacred, condemns or punishes no man without regular trial and conviction of some crime declared by antecedent laws; reprobates equally the punishment of the citizen by arbitrary acts of legislation, as by the lawless combinations of unauthorized individuals; while these men are advocates for expelling a large number of their fellow-citizens unheard, untried; or, if they cannot effect this, are for disfranchising them, in the face of the Constitution, without the judgment of their peers, and contrary to the law of the land.

The 13th article of the Constitution declares, "that no member of the State shall be *disfranchised,* or *defrauded of any of the rights* or *privileges* sacred to the subjects of this State by the Constitution, unless *by the law of the land or the judgment of his peers."* If we inquire what is meant by the law of the land, the best commentators will tell us, that it means *due process of law; that is by indictment or presentment of good and lawful men,* and trial and conviction in consequence.

* Alexander Hamilton, *A Letter from Phocion to the Considerate Citizens of New York on the Politics of the Times in Consequence of the Peace* (New York, 1784), 4, 5, 7–9, 14, 16.

It is true, that in *England,* on extraordinary occasions, attainders for high treason, by act of Parliament, have been practised; but many of the ablest advocates for civil liberty have condemned this practice; and it has commonly been exercised with great caution upon individuals only by name, never against *general descriptions* of men. The sense of our Constitution on this practice, we may gather from the 41st article, where all attainders, other than for crimes committed during the late war, are forbidden.

If there had been no treaty in the way, the Legislature might, by name, have attainted particular persons of high treason for crimes committed during the war; but, independent of the treaty, it could not, and cannot, without tyranny, disfranchise or punish whole classes of citizens by general descriptions, without trial and conviction of offences known by laws previously established, declaring the offence and prescribing the penalty.

This is a dictate of natural justice, and a fundamental principle of law and liberty.

Nothing is more common than for a free people, in times of heat and violence, to gratify momentary passions, by letting into the government, principles and precedents which afterwards prove fatal to themselves. Of this kind is the doctrine of disqualification, disfranchisement, and banishment, by acts of Legislature. The dangerous consequences of this power are manifest. If the Legislature can disfranchise any number of citizens at pleasure, by general descriptions, it may soon confine all the votes to a small number of partisans, and establish an aristocracy or an oligarchy. If it may banish at discretion all those whom particular circumstances render obnoxious, without hearing or trial, no man can be safe, nor know when he may be the innocent victim of a prevailing faction. The name of liberty applied to such a government would be a mockery of common sense. . . .

The sound and ingenious construction of the two articles, taken collectively, is this: That where the property of any persons, other than those who have been in arms against the United States, had been actually confiscated, and themselves prescribed, then Congress are to recommend a restoration of estates, rights, and properties; and, with respect to those who had been in arms, they are to recommend permission for them to remain a twelve-month in the country, to solicit a like restoration; but with respect to all those who were not in this situation, and who had not already been the objects of confiscation and banishment, they were to be absolutely secured from all future injury, to person, liberty, or property.

To say that this exemption from positive injury, does not imply a right to live among us as citizens, is a pitiful sophistry; it is to say that the banishment of a person from his country, connections, and resources (one of the greatest punishments that can befall a man), is no punishment at all.

The meaning of the word *liberty* has been contested. Its true sense must be, the enjoyment of the common privileges of subjects under the same government. There is no middle line of just construction between this sense and a mere exemption from personal imprisonment! . . .

There is a very simple and conclusive point of view in which this subject may be placed. No citizen can be deprived of any right which the citizens in general are entitled to, unless forfeited by some offence. It has been seen that the regular and constitutional mode of ascertaining whether this forfeiture has been incurred, is by legal process, trial, and conviction. This *ex vi termini* supposes prosecution. Now, consistent with the treaty, there can be no future prosecution for any thing done on account of the war. Can we then do, by act of Legislature, what the treaty disables us from doing by due course of law? This would be to imitate the Roman general, who, having promised Antiochus to restore half his vessels, caused them to be sawed in two before their delivery; or the Platœaens, who, having promised the Thebans to restore their prisoners, had them first put to death, and returned them dead.

Such fraudulent subterfuges are justly considered more odious than an open and avowed violation of treaty. . . .

The *uti possidetis, each party to hold what it possesses,* is the point from which nations set out in framing a treaty of peace. If one side gives up a part of its acquisitions, the other side renders an equivalent in some other way. What is the equivalent given to Great Britain for all the important concessions she has made? She has surrendered the capital of this State and its large dependencies. She is to surrender our immensely valuable posts on the frontier; and to yield to us a vast tract of western territory, with one half of the lakes, by which we shall command almost the whole fur trade. She renounces to us her claim to the navigation of the Mississippi, and admits us to share in the fisheries, even on better terms than we formerly enjoyed it. As she was in possession, by right of war, of all these objects, whatever may have been our original pretensions to them, they are, by the laws of nations, to be considered as so much given up on her part. And what do we give in return? We stipulate—that there shall be no future injury to her adherents among us. How insignificant the equivalent in comparison with the acquisition? . . .

The men who are at the head of the party which contends for disqualification and expulsion, endeavor to enlist a number of people on their side by holding out motives of private advantage to them. To the trader they say: "You will be overborne by the large capitals of the Tory merchants"; to the mechanic: "Your business will be less profitable, your wages less considerable, by the interference of Tory workmen." A man, the least acquainted with trade, will indeed laugh at such suggestions. . . .

These arguments, if they were understood, would be conclusive with the mechanic: "There is already employment enough for all the workmen in the city, and wages are sufficiently high. If you could raise them by expelling those who remained in the city, and whom you consider as rivals, the extravagant price of wages would have two effects; it would draw persons to settle here, not only from other parts of this State, but from the neighboring States. Those classes of the community who are to employ you, will make a great many shifts rather than pay the exorbitant prices you demand; a man will wear his old clothes so much longer, before he gets a new suit; he will buy imported shoes cheap rather than those made here at so dear a rate; the owner of a house will defer the repairs as long as possible; he will only have those which are absolutely necessary made; he will not attend to elegant improvement: and the like will happen in other branches. These circumstances will give less employment, and in a very little time bring back your wages to what they now are, and even sink them lower. But this is not all. You are not required merely to expel your rival mechanics, but you must drive away the rich merchants and others who are called Tories, to please your leaders, who will persuade you they are dangerous to your liberty (though, in fact, they only mean their own consequence). By this conduct you will drive away the principal part of those who have the means of becoming large undertakers. The carpenters and masons, in particular, must be content with patching up the houses already built, and building little huts upon the vacant lots, instead of having profitable and durable employment in erecting large and elegant edifices."

. . . The safest reliance of every government is on men's interests. This is a principle of human nature, on which all political speculation, to be just, must be founded. Make it the interest of those citizens who, during the Revolution, were opposed to us, to be friends to the new government, by affording them not only protection, but a participation in its privileges, and they will undoubtedly become its friends.

12. Toryism and Anti-Semitism: Letter in Reply to Accusations of Tory Miers Fisher, March 13, 1784*

March 13, 1784

To Miers Fisher, Esquire:

I must address you, in this manner, although you do not deserve it. Unaccustomed as you are to receive any mark of respect from the public, it will be expected that I should make an apology for introducing a character, *fetid* and *infamous*, like yours, to general notice and attention. Your conspicuous *Toryism* and *disaffection* long since buried you in the silent grave of *popular* oblivion and contempt; and your extraordinary conduct and deportment, in several other respects, has brought and re-

* *The Independent Gazetteer* (Philadelphia), March 13, 1784.

duced you to that dreary dungeon of insignificance, to that gulph of defeated spirits, from which even the powers of *hope* "that comes to all" cannot relieve or better you.

In this most miserable of all situations, principally arising from an obstinate, inflexible perseverance in your political *heresy* and *schism* (so detestable in itself, so ruinous and destructive to our country, and obnoxious to all around us), you are now left quite destitute and forlorn! Unhappy and disappointed man! Once exiled [September, 1777] and excommunicated by the state, *as a sly, insidious enemy;* severed and detached from the generous bosom of *patriotism* and *public virtue; shunned* and deserted by *faithful friends,* in whom you once so safely trusted; since, debarred and prevented from *your practice* by rule of court as an attorney at the bar; *and excluded* from every other essential and dignified privilege of which the *rest of citizens* can boast—with the wretched remains of a *wrecked* reputation— you exhibit so complete a spectacle of distress and wretchedness, as rather excites one's tenderness than vengeance, and would soften and melt down dispositions more relentless and unforgiving than mine!

But whatever claims of mercy you may demand, on these accounts; whatever I should think, were I to judge of you as your *personal* enemy in *private* respects; yet the *forward* and unexampled advances and steps you have lately taken in the concert of *public* affairs; the high-cockaded air of *fancied* importance you now assume; the petulant, discontented humor you have manifested for establishing *a new bank;* your longings and pantings to approach our *political vineyard,* and blast the fruits of those labors for which you neither *toiled nor spun;* and more particularly, the indecent, unjust, inhumane aspersions, you cast so indiscriminately on the *Jews* of this city at large, in your arguments of Wednesday week, before the honorable legislature of the commonwealth—these circumstances, if my apprehensions are right, preclude you from any lenity or favor, and present you a fair victim and offering to the sacred altar of public justice.

You are not therefore to expect any indulgence, because you merit none. I daresay you experience it not in your own feelings; nor have you any right whatever to hope for the least

tenderness from me. You shall not have it; and if you are cut
and smarted with the whip and lashes of my reproach and resentments, if I lay my talons and point out the *ingrate,* if my
tongue is clamorous of you and *your odious confederates,* and
I should pain the tenderest veins of their breasts—remember,
you first gave birth to all yourself, that it arose entirely from
you; and in tracing of events hereafter to the source you will,
perhaps, find to your sorrow and cost that you are only blame-
able for whatever consequences have or may arise on the occasion.

You not only endeavoured to injure me by your unwarrantable
expressions, but every other person of the same *religious* persuasion I hold, and which the laws of the country, and the glorious
toleration and *liberty of conscience,* have allowed me to indulge
and adopt. The injury is highly crimsoned and aggravated, as
there was no proper reason or ground for your invectives. The
attack on the *Jews* seemed wanton, and could only have been
premeditated by such a base and degenerate mind as yours. It
was not owing to the sudden sallies of passion, or to the warmth
of a disconcerted and hasty imagination. I cannot, therefore,
place it to the account of mere human frailties, in which your
will and understanding had no concern, and for which I am
always disposed to make every compassionate allowance. And
though an individual is not obliged to avenge the injuries of
particular societies and sectaries of men, he is nevertheless called upon, by every dear and serious consideration, to
speak his mind freely and independently of public consequence
and to act his part fairly on the social theatre.

Permit me, then, with this view of things, to take notice of
these terms of reproach and invective which, considering you as
a friend to good manners and decorum, you have heaped on
our nation and profession with so liberal and unsparing a
hand. I am a Jew; it is my own nation and profession. I also
subscribe myself a broker, and a broker, too, whose opportunities and knowledge, along with other brokers of his intimate ac-
quaintance, in a great course of business, has made him very
familiar and privy to every minute design and artifice of your
wiley colleagues and associates.

I exult and glory in reflecting that we have the honour to

reside in a free country where, as a people, we have met with
the most generous countenance and protection; and I do not at
all despair, notwithstanding former obstacles [the disabilities imposed by the Pennsylvania Constitution of 1776], that we shall
still obtain every other privilege that we aspire to enjoy along
with our fellow-citizens. It also affords me unspeakable satisfaction, and is indeed one of the most pleasing employments of my
thoughtful moments, to contemplate that we have in general been
early uniform, decisive Whigs, and were second to none in our
patriotism and attachment to our country!

What but Erinnys [sic—the Furies of Hell] itself could
have thus tempted you to wander from the common path of
things, and go astray among *thorns and briars?* What were your
motives and inducements for introducing the Jews so disrespect-
fully into your unhallowed and polluted lips? Who are you, or
what are you (a mere *tenant at sufferance,* of your liberty), that
in a *free* country you dare to trample on any sectary whatever
of people? Did you expect to serve yourself, or your friends and
confederates [Tories and pacifist Quakers]—these serpents in our
bosom, whose poisonous stings have been darted into every *patriot* character among us?

In any other place, in managing another cause, you might have
had patience to attend to the consequences of such unpardonable
rashness and temerity. But here you thought yourself safe, and
at full leave to take the most unlicensed liberties with characters,
in regard of whom you can in no respect pretend to vie! You
shall yet repent, even *in sackcloth* and *ashes,* for the foul language in which you have expressed yourself. And neither the
interposition of some well meant though mistaken Whigs who,
I am sorry to think, have joined you, "nor even the sacred shield
of cowardice shall protect you," for your transgressions. Who
knows but the beams of that very denomination whom you have
traduced may, on one day, perhaps not very remote, warm you
into the most abject servility, and make you penitentially solem-
nize what you have done?

An error is easily remedied, and there may be some compensation for actual injuries. But a downright insult can neither be
forgiven or forgot, and seldom admits of atonement or repara-
tion. It is our happiness to live in the times of enlightened lib-

erty, when the human mind, liberated from the restraints and fetters of superstition and authority, hath been taught to conceive just sentiments of its own; and when mankind, in matters of *religion,* are quite charitable and benevolent in their opinions of each other.

Individuals may act improperly, and sometimes deserve censure; but it is no less unjust than ungenerous to condemn all for the faults of a few, and reflect generally on a whole community for the indiscretion of some particular persons. There is no body of people but have some exceptionable characters with them; and even your own religious sectary [the Quakers], whom you have compelled me to dissect in the course of this address, are not destitute of *very proper subjects* of criticism and animadversion.

Good citizens who nauseate, and the public who contemn, have heard your invectives against the Jews. Unhappily for you, a long series of enormities have proved you more your own enemy than I am. To you, then, my worthy friends and fellow-citizens (characters teeming with strict candor and disinterestedness), do I turn myself with pleasure from the sterile field, from the *Grampian* desert, which hath hitherto employed me.

It is your candor I seek; it is your disinterestedness I solicit. The opinions of *Fisher* and his adherents, whether wilful in their malignity, or sincere in their ignorance, are no longer worthy of my notice. His observations are low; his intentions are too discernable. His whole endeavours centre in one point, namely, to create a *new bank.*

To effect this end, he has spared neither pains or labours. He has said every thing that artifice could dictate, or malice invent. He has betrayed himself in a thousand inconsistencies, and adopted absurdities which, supposing him a man of sense and observation, would have disgraced the lips of an idiot.

And for whom is the new bank meant and intended? For the benefit of men like himself, who have been in general averse and opposed to the war and common cause: for the insurgents against our liberty and independence; for *mercenary* and *artful* citizens, where selfish views are totally incompatible with the happiness of the people; for bifronted political *Janus's,* the mere weather-cocks of every breeze and gale that blows.

Who traded with the enemy? Who first depreciated the public

currency? Who lent our enemies money to carry on the war? Who were spies and pilots to the British? Who prolonged the war? Who was the cause of so many valuable men losing their lives in the field and *prisonships?* Who did not pay any taxes? Who has now the public securities in hand? Who would not receive our Continental money? Who has purchased *Burgoyne's* convention bills? Who depreciated the French bills? Who depreciated the bills of the *United States* on Paris? Who slandered the institution of the *Bank* of *North-America?* Who refused taking *banknotes* when they fi[r]st issued? Who discouraged the people from lodging money in the bank? And are these the characters who talk of instituting a bank for *the good of the public?* Are these the people who want a charter from our legislature? Shall such a bastard progeny of freedom, such jests and phantoms of patriotism and the social virtues be indulged in their wishes? For shame! For shame! Surrender the puerile, the fruitless pretensions! Public honor and public gratitude cry aloud against you, and says, or seems to say, as earnest as your endeavors have been, you shall not have your charter.

From such a *medley* and *group* of characters (an impure nest of vipers, the very *bloodhounds* of our lives and liberties) we have every thing to hazard, and nothing to expect. Suspicion shakes her wary head against them, and experience suggests that the sly, insinuating intrigues and combinations of these persons are to be watched and guarded against as much as possible. Though the *proposals* are generous and captivating, their practices, I will venture to affirm, cannot correspond; and however *fascinating* they may be *in appearance,* their designs are *deep* and *wiley*. With the soft and soothing voice of *Jacob* they may exercise the *hand,* the *hairy* hand of Esau!

I shall not inquire whether two banks in a commercial country would not clash with each other, and prove exceeding detrimental and injurious to the community. Having only ventured to give an account of the leading characters who compose the new bank, allow me in conclusion to rectify an error of Mr. Fisher's, who publicly declared, "the Jews were the authors of high and unusual interest." No! The Jews can acquit themselves of this artful imputation, and turn your own batteries on yourself. It was neither the *Jews* or *Christians* that founded the practice, but

Quakers—and *Quakers* worse than *heathens, pagans,* or *idolaters;* men, though not Jews in *faith,* are yet Jews in *traffic;* men abounding with avarice, *who neither fear God, nor regard man.*

Those very persons who are now flattering themselves with the idea of a new bank, first invented the practise of discounting notes at five per cent. I have retained an alphabetical list of names, as well as the other brokers, and can specify persons, if necessary. In the language of Naphtali to David, I have it in my power to point at the very *would-be* directors, and say: *"Thou art the man."* I can prove that it were these people, unwilling to venture money in trade during the war, who first declined letting out money on the best mortgage and bond security.

Were they now gratified in their expectations, would they not display the same undue spirit and degrade the dignity of a bank with practices unbecoming a common broker? Is it not in their power to finess at the bank, and refuse discounting notes on purpose to gripe the necessitous part of the people, and extort improper premiums out of doors? And have we not reason to expect this would be the case?

A JEW BROKER

Chapter V

THE FRONTIER POSTS

On April 8, 1784, Lord Sydney, the Secretary of State for Home Affairs in the Pitt government, instructed the Governor-General of Canada not to withdraw the garrisons from the frontier posts on the ground that no definite time for such withdrawal was fixed in the Treaty of 1783. The pretext for the British action was the failure of the Americans to comply with the provisions of the Treaty regarding the collection of debts and the confiscation of Loyalist estates. As Jay wrote John Adams at London, "They hold the posts but they will hold them as pledges of enmity; and the time must come when the seeds of discontent, resentment and hatred, which such measures always sow, will produce bitter fruit." Meantime, it is clear that Loyalist and Canadian officials sought to exploit Indian discontent in order to keep the British foothold in the West, confident that the internal weaknesses in the Confederation would prevent the United States from taking military action. Such a view was expressed in the following letter from a Loyalist leader to an Indian Chief.

13.   Loyalist Incitement of the Indians, Sir John Johnson to Captain Joseph Brant, March 22, 1787 *

Quebec, March 22d, 1787

Dear Sir,

I have received your letter of the 14th February. I am happy to find things turned out as you wished at your several meetings in the Indian country near Detroit, and I hope it may have the effect you wish in preventing the American from incroaching on your lands. Your conduct, I hope, for your own sake, will always be such as to justify the good opinion that has been entertained of you by your friends the English, and such as will merit the continuance of their friendship. I hope in all your decisions you will conduct yourselves with prudence and moderation, having always an eye to the friendship that has so long subsisted between you and the King's subjects, upon whom alone you can and ought to depend. You have no reason to fear any breach of promise on the part of the King. Is he not every year giving fresh proofs of his friendship? What greater could you expect than is now about to be performed, by giving an ample compensation for your losses, which is yet withheld from us, his subjects? Do not suffer bad men or evil advisers to lead you astray; every thing that is reasonable and consistent with the friendship that ought to be preserved between us, will be done for you all. Do not suffer an idea to hold a place in your mind, that it will be for your interests to sit still and see the Americans attempt the posts. It is for your sakes chiefly, if not entirely,

* W. F. Stone, *Life of Joseph Brant,* 2 vols. (New York, 1838), II, 268–269.

that we hold them. If you become indifferent about them, they may perhaps be given up; what security would you then have? You would be left at the mercy of a people whose blood calls aloud for revenge; whereas, by supporting them, you encourage us to hold them, and encourage the new settlements, already considerable, and every day increasing by numbers coming in, who find they can't live in the States. Many thousands are preparing to come in. This increase of his Majesty's subjects will serve as a protection for you, should the subjects of the States, by endeavoring to make farther encroachments on you, disturb your quiet. At present I think there is little to apprehend from any but the Southern States; those to the eastward are already opposed to each other in arms, and have shed blood, and the disorder seems to be spreading throughout. Men of character are coming in here to see if no assistance will be given them; and the people of New England, who were the most violent at the commencement of the war, are now the most desirous of returning under the British government, should Great Britain incline to receive them, which many think they would not.

Remember me in the most friendly manner to Mrs. Brant, all your family, and to all my brothers in your settlement, and tell them to be patient, and that they will find that all that has been promised them, coming within my knowledge, will be performed. I hope to see you in the course of the summer; in the mean time, I remain with truth,

Dear Sir,

> Your friend and
> Humble servant,
> JOHN JOHNSON

Chapter VI

THE WINDS OF ECONOMIC CHANGE

One of the major economic developments in the post-Revolutionary period was the change in the direction of American trade. Old markets like the British West Indies were cut off to American ships by the British Orders in Council, while commerce with the French and the Dutch was being rapidly expanded. However, the event that had the greatest long-range consequences was the opening of trade with the Orient. The first American ship to reach the Far East was the Empress of China, *whose historic voyage in 1784–85 was chronicled by Major Samuel Shaw, agent for the owners of the vessel.*

Another important economic development of the Confederation period was the establishment of banking facilities. For many years merchants had wanted banks which would provide capital as well as other banking functions. Foremost among these institutions, if not the very first, was the Bank of North America, chartered by Congress at the instigation of financier Robert Morris in 1781. Besides serving private enterprise the Bank also provided certain central banking functions such as loaning money to the central government. Although the Bank never assumed the stature that its supporters had hoped for (see Morris' statement below), it did stand as a model for future banks—especially the First Bank of the United States.

While Americans rechanneled their foreign trade in the post-Revolutionary period, they also undertook commercial changes at home. Manufacturing grew at an unprecedented scale. More business enterprises were started during this era than in any previous one. Societies were formed and articles were written for the purpose of encouraging manufacture. In the essay below William Barton, Revolutionary War veteran and later a Federalist, argued that the United States could never achieve full independence and national integrity unless it was economically independent.

14.   China Trade: Samuel Shaw to John Jay, May 19, 1785*

Samuel Shaw to Jay.

New York, 19th May, 1785.

Sir:

The first vessel that has been fitted out by the inhabitants of the United States of America for essaying a commerce with those of the empire of China, being, by the favour of Heaven, safe returned to this port, it becomes my duty to communicate to you, for the information of the fathers of the country, an account of the reception their Citizens have met with, and the respect with which their flag has been treated in that distant region; especially as some circumstances have occurred which had a tendency to attract the attention of the Chinese towards a people of whom they have hitherto had but very confused Ideas, and which serve in a peculiar manner, place the Americans in a more conspicuous point of view, than has commonly attended the introduction of other Nations into that ancient and extensive Empire.

The Ship employed on this occasion is about three hundred and sixty tons burthen, built in America and equipped with forty-three persons, under the command of John Green, Esq.

* H. P. Johnston (ed.), *Correspondence and Public Papers of John Jay,* 4 vols. (New York, 1890–93), III, 144–149.

The subscriber had the honor of being appointed agent for their Commerce by the Gentlemen, at whose risk this first experiment has been undertaken.

On the 22 of Feby., 1784, the Ship sailed from New York, and arrived the 21 March at St. Iago, the principal of the Cape de Verd islands. Having paid our respects to the Portuguese viceroy, and with his permission taken such refreshments as were necessary, we left those islands on the 27th, and pursued our voyage. After a pleasant passage, in which nothing extraordinary occurred, we came to anchor in the straits of Sunda on the 18th July. It was no small addition to our happiness on this occasion to meet there two ships belonging to our good allies the French. The commodore, Monsieur D'Ordelin, and his officers, welcomed us in the most affectionate manner; and as his own ship was immediately bound to Canton, gave us an invitation to go in company with him. This friendly offer we most cheerfully accepted, and the commodore furnished us with his signals by day and night, and added such instructions for our passage through the Chinese seas as would have been exceedingly beneficial had any unfortunate accident occasioned our separation. Happily, we pursued our route together. On our arrival at the island of Macao, the French consul for China, Monsieur Vieillard, with some other gentlemen of his nation, came on board to congratulate and welcome us to that part of the world; and kindly undertook the introduction of the Americans to the Portuguese governor. The little time that we were there was entirely taken up by the good offices of the consul, the gentlemen of his nation, and those of the Swedes and Imperialists who still remained at Macao. The other Europeans had repaired to Canton. Three days afterward we finished our outward-bound voyage. Previous to coming to anchor, we saluted the shipping in the river with thirteen guns, which were answered by the several commodores of the European nations, each of whom sent an officer to compliment us on our arrival. These visits were returned by the captain and supercargoes in the afternoon; who were again saluted by the respective ships as they finished their visit. When the French sent their officers to congratulate us, they added to the obligations we were already under to them, by furnishing men, boats, and anchors to assist us in coming to safe and convenient moorings. Nor did their good offices stop here; they insisted further that until we were settled, we should take up our quarters with them at Canton.

The day of our arrival at Canton, August 30, and the two following days, we were visited by the Chinese merchants, and the chiefs and gentlemen of the several European establishments. The Chinese were very indulgent towards us. They styled us the *new people;* and when by the map we conveyed to them an idea of the extent of our country, with its present and increasing population, they were highly pleased at the prospect of so considerable a market for the productions of theirs.

The situation of the Europeans at Canton is so well known as to render a detail unnecessary. The good understanding commonly subsisting between them and the Chinese was in some degree interrupted by two extraordinary occurrences; of which I will, with your permission, give a particular account.

The police at Canton is at all times extremely strict, and the Europeans residing there are circumscribed within very narrow limits. The latter had observed with concern some circumstances which they deemed an encroachment upon their rights. On this consideration they determined to apply for redress to the *hoppo,* who is the head officer of the customs, the next time he should visit the shipping. Deputies accordingly attended from every nation, and I was desired to represent ours. We met the hoppo on board an English ship, and the causes of complaint were soon after removed.

The other occurrence, of which I beg leave to take notice, gave rise to what was commonly called the *Canton war,* which threatened to be productive of very serious consequences. On the 25th November an English ship in saluting some company that had dined on board, killed a Chinese, and wounded two others in the mandarin's boat alongside.

It is a maxim of the Chinese law that blood must answer for blood; in pursuance of which they demanded the unfortunate gunner. To give up this poor man was to consign him to certain death. Humanity pleaded powerfully against the measure. After repeated conferences between the English and the Chinese, the latter declared themselves satisfied, and the affair was supposed to be entirely settled. Notwithstanding this, on the morning after the last conference (the 27th), the supercargo of the ship was seized while attending his business, thrown into a sedan-chair, hurried into the city, and committed to prison.

Such an outrage on personal liberty spread a general alarm; and the Europeans unanimously agreed to send for their boats, with armed men from the shipping, for the security of themselves and property until the matter should be brought to a conclusion. The boats accordingly came, and ours among the number; one of which was fired on, and a man wounded. All trade was stopped, and the Chinese men-of-war drawn up opposite the factories. The Europeans demanded the restoration of Mr. Smith, which the Chinese refused, until the gunner should be given up.

In the mean while the troops of the province were collecting in the neighborhood of Canton—the Chinese servants were ordered by the magistrates to leave the factories—the gates of the suburbs were shut—all intercourse was at an end—the naval force was increased—many troops were embarked in boats, ready for landing—and every thing wore the appearance of war. To what extremities matters might have been carried, had not a negotiation taken place, no one can say. The Chinese asked a conference with all the nations except the English. A deputation (in which I was included for America) met the *Fuen,* who is the head magistrate of Canton, with the principal officers of the province. After setting forth, by an interpreter, the power of the emperor and his own determination to support the laws, he demanded that the gunner should be given up within three days, declaring that he should have an impartial examination before their tribunal, and if it appeared that the affair was accidental, he should be released unhurt.

In the mean time he gave permission for the trade, excepting that of the English, to go on as usual; and dismissed us with a present of two pieces of silk to each, as a mark of his friendly disposition. The other nations, one after another, sent away their boats under protection of *a Chinese flag,* and pursued their business as before. The English were obliged to submit, the gunner was given up, Mr. Smith was released, and the English, after being forced to ask pardon of the magistracy of Canton in presence of the other nations, had their commerce restored.

On this occasion I am happy that we were the last who sent off our boat, and that *without a Chinese flag;* nor did she go till the English themselves thanked us for our concurrence with them, and advised the sending her away. After peace was restored, the chief and four English gentlemen visited the several nations (among whom we were included), and thanked them for their assistance during the troubles. The gunner remained with the Chinese, his fate undetermined.

Notwithstanding the treatment we received from all parties was perfectly civil and respectful, yet it was with peculiar satisfaction that we experienced on every occasion from our good allies the French the most flattering and substantial proofs of their friendship. "If," said they, "we have in any instance been serviceable to you, we are happy; and we desire nothing more ardently than further opportunities to convince you of our affection."

We left Canton the 27th December, and on our return refreshed at the Cape of Good Hope, where we found a most friendly reception. After remaining there five days, we sailed for America, and arrived in this port on the 11th instant.

To every lover of his country, as well as to those more immediately concerned in commerce, it must be a pleasing reflection that a communication is thus happily opened between us and the eastern extremity of the globe; and it adds very sensibly to the pleasure of this reflection, that the voyage has been performed in so short a space of time, and attended with the loss only of one man. To Captain Green and his officers every commendation is due, for their unwearied and successful endeavours in bringing it to this most fortunate issue, which fully justifies the confidence reposed in them by the gentlemen concerned in the enterprise.

Permit me, sir, to accompany this letter with the two pieces of silk presented to me by the *Fuen* of Canton, as a mark of his good disposition towards the American nation. In that view I consider myself as peculiarly honoured, in being charged with this testimony of the friendship of the Chinese, for a people who may in a few years prosecute a commerce with the subjects of

that empire under advantages equal, if not superior, to those
enjoyed by any other nation whatever.

I have the honour to be,

With the most perfect respect, sir,

Your most obedient and very humble servant,

SAMUEL SHAW.

15. Development of Banking: Robert Morris' Announcement of the Opening of the Bank of North America, January 8, 1782*

I HAVE the honor to transmit herewith an ordinance passed by
the United States in Congress assembled the 31st day of December, 1781, incorporating the subscribers of the Bank of
North America, together with sundry resolutions recommending
to the several states to pass such laws as they may judge necessary for giving the said ordinance its full operation. The resolutions of the 26th of May last speak so clearly to the points
necessary to be established by those laws, that I need not enlarge
on them. Should anything more be found necessary upon experience, the President and Directors will no doubt make suitable applications to Congress, or to the states respectively, as
the case may require.

It affords me great satisfaction to inform you that this Bank
commenced its operations yesterday, and I am confident that
with proper management, it will answer the most sanguine expectations of those who befriend the institution. It will facilitate
the management of the finances of the United States. The several states may, when their respective necessities require, and

* J. Sparks (ed.), *Diplomatic Correspondence of the American Revolution,* 12 vols. (Boston, 1829–30), XII, 76–77.

the abilities of the bank will permit, derive occasional advantages and accommodations from it. It will afford to the individuals of all the states a medium for their intercourse with each other, and for the payment of taxes more convenient than the precious metals, and equally safe. It will have a tendency to increase both the internal and external commerce of North America, and undoubtedly will be infinitely useful to all the traders of every state in the Union, provided, as I have already said, it is conducted on principles of equity, justice, prudence, and economy. The present directors bear characters, which cannot fail to inspire confidence, and as the corporation is amenable to the laws, power can neither sanctify any improper conduct, nor protect the guilty.

16. Encouragement of Manufacturing: William Barton's Essay on the Promotion of Manufacture, September 1787 *

Essay on the promotion of American manufactures
By William Barton, esq.

Every man must be convinced that a people, who have resource to foreign markets for almost every article of their consumption, can be independent in name only; and are incapable, under such circumstances, of becoming either great or prosperous. There is not, perhaps, any nation that is rendered so dependent, by nature. And yet, how extraordinary is it, that this country, to which providence has been peculiarly bountiful, in the distribution of those things that contribute to the convenience, ease, and happiness of man, should unnecessarily and wantonly

* *American Museum* (Philadelphia), II, no. 3 (September 1787), 257–258.

give a preference to foreign commodities, although at the expence of the most important interests of the government and individuals! There is no country possessing greater natural advantages: and, consequently, no nation can be more respectable and happy than the united states may become, by a proper improvement of those advantages: but, to make the most of them, we must practise the virtues of industry and economy—virtues essential to the well-being of a republic. Our governments must also promote the introduction of useful manufactures and trades among us; and protect such as are already instituted. Thus we shall employ and enrich our own citizens; accelerate the population of an extensive and valuable country; and increase our national strength, dignity, and independence.

If we take a view of the various articles of trade and commerce, which our country supplies, and of the numerous and profitable manufactures and employments, which may be established in the several states, under due encouragement, we shall be convinced we may become, in a few years, a thriving, happy, and truly independent people. Previous to the late revolution, it was a favourite sentiment among Englishmen, and an opinion imbibed by too many Americans, that it was contrary to the interest of this country to carry on manufactures. However just the observation might have appeared to Englishmen, when applied to us as colonists, and a subordinate part of the British empire, it is totally inapplicable to us as a sovereign and distinct power. All the principal advantages that Europeans can derive from manufactures and mechanic arts, may be obtained by their introduction here. The inhabitants of America are supposed to double their numbers every twenty years: what, then, is to become of this vast increase of the inhabitants of our towns? They cannot be all labourers: and but a small part can engage in husbandry, the learned professions, or merchandize: consequently, the greater part must apply to trades and manufactures, or starve. Besides, it is to be supposed, that a very considerable proportion of the emigrants from Europe, hither, will be tradesmen, who are neither capable nor desirous of becoming farmers: and, in proportion to the encouragement manufactures receive, will be the accession of tradesmen and mechanics to us, from abroad.

Labour is dear in America, because the lands are thinly settled, in proportion to their extent: and this has been urged as a powerful reason, why we cannot manufacture to advantage. But it ought to be considered, that as population increases, (and this, it has been observed, is very rapidly), the price of labour will fall: and that, altho' our manufactures may, for some years to come, be higher than foreign ones, yet, as the price of the former would be paid to our own citizens, and that money be kept in the country, which would otherwise leave it, to return no more—we might thereby be better enabled to pay the advanced price for our own, than somewhat less for foreign commodities. It is, at any rate, our interest, as a nation, to support those manufactures, in the first place, which are produced from the native productions and raw materials of the country, or from such as may be easily procured, and which require not much labour in proportion to the value. Many of the smaller kind might employ numbers of industrious poor, unfit for hard labour, and likewise women and children.

Chapter VII

THE WINDS OF REFORM

One of the major reforms of the Confederation period was the abolition of slavery or the adoption of gradual emancipation in several northern states. Though the movement had little success in the South, there was an attempt made in Virginia to bring about the ultimate extinction of slavery. In a bill drafted by Thomas Jefferson in 1779 and passed in amended form in 1785, one sees the germ of an emancipation scheme. Furthermore, as indicated in his Notes on Virginia *(see below), an amendment was proposed to emancipate all slaves born after the passage of the act, but this was not adopted.*

Another significant development in the movement to end slavery was the establishment of manumission societies. These organizations were formed for the purpose of encouraging individuals to emancipate their slaves, to work for the passage of laws easing restrictions on manumission, and to aid free Negroes. The first such society was founded in Philadelphia in 1775, but it was not until the 1780's that the movement really expanded, as twelve more groups were formed. John Jay, president of the New York Society, in the letter below, describes the difficulties involved in advancing the cause and alludes to some of the accomplishments of his organization.

The movement for religious liberty begun during the American Revolution made its greatest gain in the Confederation period. This was the achievement of separation of church and state in Virginia. An ordinance for religious freedom had been proposed by Thomas Jefferson in 1779, but it had been rejected by the Virginia legislature. However, during Jefferson's tour of duty as minister to France, largely through the efforts of James Madison, George Mason, and a few others, the bill was finally passed. Jefferson considered the statute for religious freedom one of his three greatest accomplishments, along with the Declaration of Independence and the establishment of the University of Virginia. A foreign commentator, the French Chargé d'Affaires, casts illumination on the position of the Jews, Catholics, and dissenting sects in this period.

Penal reform was another field in which progress was achieved during the Confederation period. In 1787, a number of leading philanthropists, including Benjamin Rush and Tench Coxe, established the Philadelphia Society for Alleviating the Miseries of Public Prisons. The organization's objective was to have prisons investigated and to suggest improvements in discipline and penal method. The essay, read by Dr. Rush at a meeting of the group, emphasized that public punishments were detrimental to the criminal and to society. Three years later, the state of Pennsylvania adopted a new system of prison discipline embodying many of the Society's proposals.

17. Thomas Jefferson's Bill Concerning Slaves, June 18, 1779, and Comments Upon Slavery from *Notes on Virginia*, 1782*

A Bill concerning Slaves

Be it enacted by the General Assembly, that no persons shall, henceforth, be slaves within this commonwealth, except such as were so on the first day of this present session of Assembly, and the descendants of the females of them.

Negroes and mulattoes which shall hereafter be brought into this commonwealth and kept therein one whole year, together, or so long at different times as shall amount to one year, shall be free. [But if they shall not depart the commonwealth within

* P. F. Ford (ed.), *Writings of Thomas Jefferson,* 10 vols. (New York, 1892–99), II, 201–203; III, 243–244.

one year thereafter they shall be out of the protection of the laws.

Those which shall come into this commonwealth of their own accord shall be out of the protection of the laws; save only such as being seafaring persons and navigating vessels hither, shall not leave the same while here more than twenty four hours together.

It shall not be lawful for any person to emancipate a slave but by deed executed, proved and recorded as is required by law in the case of a conveyance of goods and chattels, on consideration not deemed valuable in law, or by last will and testament, and with the free consent of such slave, expressed in presence of the court of the county wherein he resides: And if such slave, so emancipated, shall not within one year thereafter, depart the commonwealth, he shall be out of the protection of the laws. All conditions, restrictions and limitations annexed to any act of emancipation shall be void from the time such emancipation is to take place.

If any white woman shall have a child by a negro or mulatto, she and her child shall depart the commonwealth within one year thereafter. If they fail so to do, the woman shall be out of the protection of the laws, and the child shall be bound out by the Aldermen of the county, in like manner as poor orphans are by law directed to be, and within one year after its term of service expired shall depart the commonwealth, or on failure so to do, shall be out of the protection of the laws.

Where any of the persons before described shall be disabled from departing the commonwealth by grievous sickness, the protection of the law shall be continued to him until such disability be removed: And if the county shall in the mean time, incur any expence in taking care of him, as of other county poor, the Aldermen shall be intitled to recover the same from his former master, if he had one, his heirs, executors and administrators.]

No negro or mulatto shall be a witness except in pleas of the commonwealth against negroes or mullatoes, or in civil pleas wherein negroes or mullattoes alone shall be parties.

No slave shall go from the tenements of his master, or other person with whom he lives, without a pass, or some letter or token whereby it may appear that he is proceeding by authority from his master, employer, or overseer: If he does, it shall be lawful for any person to apprehend and carry him before a Justice of the Peace, to be by his order punished with stripes, or not, in his discretion.

No slave shall keep any arms whatever, nor pass, unless with written orders from his master or employer, or in his company, with arms from one place to another. Arms in possession of a slave contrary to this prohibition shall be forefeited to him who will seize them.

Riots, routs, unlawful assemblies, trespasses and seditious speeches by a negro or mulatto shall be punished with stripes at the discretion of a Justice of the Peace; and he who will may apprehend and carry him before such Justice.

From Notes on Virginia:

To emancipate all slaves born after the passing the act. The bill reported by the revisers does not itself contain this proposition; but an amendment containing it was prepared, to be offered to the legislature whenever the bill should be taken up, and farther directing, that they should continue with their parents to a certain age, then to be brought up, at the public expense, to tillage, arts, or sciences, according to their geniuses, till the females should be eighteen, and the males twenty-one years of age, when they should be colonized to such place as the circumstances of the time should render most proper, sending them out with arms, implements of household and of the handicraft arts, seeds, pairs of the useful domestic animals, &c., to declare them a free and independent people, and extend to them our alliance and protection, till they have acquired strength; and to send vessels at the same time to other parts of the world for an equal number of white inhabitants; to induce them to migrate hither, proper encouragements were to be proposed.

18. Establishment of the Anti-Slavery Movement: John Jay, President of the New York Manumission Society, to the English Anti-Slavery Society, June, 1788*

Jay to the English Anti-Slavery Society

Gentlemen:

Our society has been favoured with your letter of the 1st of May last, and are happy that efforts so honourable to the nation are making in your country to promote the cause of justice and humanity relative to the Africans. That they who know the value of liberty, and are blessed with the enjoyment of it, ought not to subject others to slavery, is, like most other moral precepts, more generally admitted in theory than observed in practice. This will continue to be too much the case while men are impelled to action by their passions rather than their reason, and while they are more solicitous to acquire wealth than to do as they would be done by. Hence it is that India and Africa experience unmerited oppression from nations which have long been distinguished by their attachment to their civil and religious liberties, but who have expended not much less blood and treasure in violating the rights of others than in defending their own. The United States are far from being irreproachable in this respect. It undoubtedly is very inconsistent with their declarations on the subject of human rights to permit a single slave to be found within their jurisdiction, and we confess the justice of your strictures on that head.

Permit us, however, to observe, that although consequences

* H. P. Johnston, *Correspondence and Public Papers of John Jay*, III, 340–344.

ought not to deter us from doing what is right, yet that it is not easy to persuade men in general to act on that magnanimous and disinterested principle. It is well known that errors, either in opinion or practice, long entertained or indulged, are difficult to eradicate, and particularly so when they have become, as it were, incorporated in the civil institutions and domestic economy of a whole people.

Prior to the great revolution, the great majority or rather the great body of our people had been so long accustomed to the practice and convenience of having slaves, that very few among them even doubted the propriety and rectitude of it. Some liberal and conscientious men had, indeed, by their conduct and writings, drawn the lawfulness of slavery into question, and they made converts to that opinion; but the number of those converts compared with the people at large was then very inconsiderable. Their doctrines prevailed by almost insensible degrees, and was like the little lump of leaven which was put into three measures of meal: even at this day, the whole mass is far from being leavened, though we have good reason to hope and to believe that if the natural operations of truth are constantly watched and assisted, but not forced and precipitated, that end we all aim at will finally be attained in this country.

The Convention which formed and recommended the new Constitution had an arduous task to perform, especially as local interests, and in some measure local prejudices, were to be accommodated. Several of the States conceived that restraints on slavery might be too rapid to consist with their particular circumstances; and the importance of union rendered it necessary that their wishes on that head should, in some degree, be gratified.

It gives us pleasure to inform you, that a disposition favourable to our views and wishes prevails more and more, and that it has already had an influence on our laws. When it is considered how many of the legislators in the different States are proprietors of slaves, and what opinions and prejudices they have imbibed on the subject from their infancy, a sudden and total stop to this species of oppression is not to be expected.

We will cheerfully co-operate with you in endeavouring to procure advocates for the same cause in other countries, and perfectly approve and commend your establishing a correspondence in France. It appears to have produced the desired effect; for Mons. De Varville, the secretary of a society for the like benevolent purpose at Paris, is now here, and comes instructed to establish a correspondence with us, and to collect such information as may promote our common views. He delivered to our society an extract from the minutes of your proceedings, dated 8th of April last, recommending him to our attention, and upon that occasion they passed the resolutions of which the enclosed are copies.

We are much obliged by the pamphlets enclosed with your letter, and shall constantly make such communications to you as may appear to us interesting.

By a report of the committee for superintending the school we have established in this city for the education of negro children, we find that proper attention is paid to it, and that scholars are now taught in it. By the laws of this State, masters may now liberate healthy slaves of a proper age without giving security that they shall not become a parish charge; and the exportation as well as importation of them is prohibited. The State has also manumitted such as became its property by confiscation; and we have reason to expect that the maxim, that every man, of whatever colour, is to be presumed to be free until the contrary is shown, will prevail in our courts of justice. Manumissions daily become more common among us; and the treatment which slaves in general meet with in this State is very little different from that of other servants.

I have the honour to be, gentlemen,

Your humble servant,

JOHN JAY

President of the Society for Promoting the Manumission of Slaves

19. Virginia Statute of Religious Liberty, January 16, 1786 *

An Act for establishing Religious Freedom

I. WHEREAS Almighty God hath created the mind free; that all attempts to influence it by temporal punishments or burthens, or by civil incapacitations, tend only to beget habits of hypocrisy and meanness, and are a departure from the plan of the Holy author of our religion, who being Lord both of body and mind, yet chose not to propagate it by coercions on either, as was in his Almighty power to do; that the impious presumption of legislators and rulers, civil as well as ecclesiastical, who being themselves but fallible and uninspired men, have assumed dominion over the faith of others, setting up their own opinions and modes of thinking as the only true and infallible, and as such endeavouring to impose them on others, hath established and maintained false religions over the greatest part of the world, and through all time; that to compel a man to furnish contributions of money for the propagation of opinions which he disbelieves, is sinful and tyrannical; that even the forcing him to support this or that teacher of his own religious persuasion, is depriving him of the comfortable liberty of giving his contributions to the particular pastor whose morals he would make his pattern, and whose powers he feels most persuasive to righteousness, and is withdrawing from the ministry those temporary rewards, which proceeding from an approbation of their personal

* W. W. Hening (ed.), *Statutes at Large . . . of Virginia,* 13 vols. (Richmond, 1819–23), XII, 84 *et seq.*

conduct, are an additional incitement to earnest and unremitting labours for the instruction of mankind; that our civil rights have no dependence on our religious opinions, any more than our opinions in physics or geometry; that therefore the proscribing any citizen as unworthy the public confidence by laying upon him an incapacity of being called to offices of trust and emolument, unless he profess or renounce this or that religious opinion, is depriving him injuriously of those privileges and advantages to which in common with his fellow-citizens he has a natural right, that it tends only to corrupt the principles of that religion it is meant to encourage, by bribing with a monopoly of worldly honours and emoluments, those who will externally profess and conform to it; that though indeed these are criminal who do not withstand such temptation, yet neither are those innocent who lay the bait in their way; that to suffer the civil magistrate to intrude his powers into the field of opinion, and to restrain the profession or propagation of principles on supposition of their ill tendency, is a dangerous fallacy, which at once destroys all religious liberty, because he being of course judge of that tendency will make his opinions the rule of judgment, and approve or condemn the sentiments of others only as they shall square with or differ from his own; that it is time enough for the rightful purposes of civil government, for its officers to interfere when principles break out into overt acts against peace and good order; and finally, that truth is great and will prevail if left to herself, that she is the proper and sufficient antagonist to error, and has nothing to fear from the conflict, unless by human interposition disarmed of her natural weapons, free argument and debate, errors ceasing to be dangerous when it is permitted freely to contradict them.

II. *Be it enacted by the General Assembly,* that no man shall be compelled to frequent or support any religious worship, place or ministry whatsoever, nor shall be enforced, restrained, molested, or burthened in his body or goods, nor shall otherwise suffer on account of his religious opinions or belief; but that all men shall be free to profess, and by argument to maintain, their opinion in matters of religion, and that the same shall in no wise diminish, enlarge or affect their civil capacities.

III. And though we well know that this assembly, elected by

the people for the ordinary purposes of legislation only, have no power to restrain the acts of succeeding assemblies, constituted with powers equal to our own, and that therefore to declare this act to be irrevocable would be of no effect in law; yet as we are free to declare, and do declare, that the rights hereby asserted are of the natural rights of mankind, and that if any act shall hereafter be passed to repeal the present, or to narrow its operation, such act will be an infringement of natural right.

20.   Religious Liberty and the Jews: French Chargé d'Affaires Chevalier Louis-Guillaume Otto to Foreign Minister Comte de Vergennes, January 2, 1786*

All Christian sects enjoy in America an entire liberty. The Jews have the exercise of their religion only; but they make efforts to enter into the legislative assemblies. It would be very remarkable if this people, after having suffered the contempt of all ages and nations, should succeed in America in taking part in the affairs of government. But this revolution is not yet ripe; and although, according to the terms of several of the constitutions, it is enough to recognise a God to enter the assembly, prejudices are still too strong to enable the Jews to enjoy the privileges accorded to all their fellow-citizens. But whatever may be the tolerance of the different states in the United States, religious zeal awakens so soon as one sect dares to take the lead over another. The Presbyterians of Pennsylvania and Massachusetts have not yet been reconciled to the Anglicans; and when a preacher announces some exaggerated pretensions, it is enough to inflame the op-

* George Bancroft, *History of the Formation of the Constitution of the United States of America,* 3rd ed., 2 vols. (New York, 1883), I, 476–477.

posite party. The small number of Catholics have not yet given umbrage; but it is believed here, as in England, that this religion is contrary to political liberty; and, if it is augmented by the aid of any foreign power, they will not fail to oppose its increase with vivacity. Moreover, we are essentially interested that there should not be in America a French church, since it would be one motive the more to excite the subjects of his Majesty to emigrate. Mr. de la Valinière assembles the French who are in his house. He preaches regularly to them every Sunday, and he assured me that he is persuaded that, if there were a French church here, it would, without doubt, attract a great number of his countrymen.

21. Prison and Penal Reform: Benjamin Rush's Enquiry into the Effects of Public Punishments Upon Criminals and Upon Society, March 9, 1787 *

The design of punishment is said to be, first, to reform the person who suffers it, secondly, to prevent the perpetration of crimes, by exciting terror in the minds of spectators; and, thirdly, to remove those persons from society, who have manifested, by their tempers and crimes, that they are unfit to live in it.

From the first institution of governments, in every age and country (with only a few exceptions) legislators have thought that punishments should be *public*, in order to produce the two first of these intentions. It will require some fortitude to combat opinions that have been sanctified by such long and general prejudice, and supported by universal practice. But truth in government, as well as in philosophy, is of progressive growth.

* B. Rush, *An Enquiry into the Effects of Public Punishments Upon Criminals and Upon Society* (Philadelphia, 1787).

As in philosophy, we often arrive at truth by rejecting the evidence of our senses; so in government, we often arrive at it after divorcing our first thoughts. Reason, tho' deposed and oppressed, is the only just sovereign of the human mind. Discoveries, it is true, have been made by accident; but they have derived their credit and usefulness only from their according with the decisions of reason.

In medicine, above every other branch of philosophy, we perceive many instances of the want of relation between the apparent cause and effect. Who, by reasoning a priori, would suppose, that the hot regimen was not preferable to the cold, in the treatment of the small-pox? But experience teaches us, that this is not the case. Cause and effect appear to be related in philosophy, like the objects of chymistry. Similar bodies often repel each other, while bodies that are dissimilar in figure, weight and quality, often unite together with impetuosity. With our present imperfect degrees of knowledge of the properties of bodies, we can discover these chymical relations only by experiment. The same may be said of the connection between *cause* and *effect,* in many parts of government. This connection often accords with reason, while it is repugnant to our senses—and when this is not the case, from our inability to perceive it, it forces our consent from the testimony of experience and observation.

It has been remarked, that the profession of arms owes its present rank, as a science, to its having been rescued, since the revival of letters, from the hands of mere soldiers, and cultivated by men acquainted with other branches of literature. The reason of this is plain. Truth is an unit. It is the same thing in war-philosophy-medicine-morals-religion and government; and in proportion as we arrive at it in one science, we shall discover it in others.

After this apology, for dissenting from the established opinions and practice, upon the subject of public punishments, I shall take the liberty of declaring, that the great ends proposed, are not to be obtained by them; and that, on the contrary, all *public* punishments tend to make bad men worse, and to encrease crimes, by their influence upon society.

I. The reformation of a criminal can never be effected by a public punishment, for the following reasons:

1st, As it is always connected with infamy, it destroys in him the sense of shame, which is one of the strongest out-posts of virtue.

2ndly, It is generally of such short duration, as to produce none of those changes in body or mind, which are absolutely necessary to reform obstinate habits of vice.

3rdly, Experience proves, that public punishments have encreased propensities to crimes. A man who has lost his character at a whipping-post, has nothing valuable left to lose in society. Pain has begotten insensibility to the whip; and shame to infamy. Added to his old habits of vice, he probably feels a spirit of revenge against the whole community, whose laws have inflicted his punishment upon him; and hence he is stimulated, to add to the number and enormity of his outrages upon society. The long duration of the punishment, when public, by encreasing its infamy, serves only to encrease the evils that have been mentioned. The criminals, who were sentenced to work in the presence of the city of London, upon the Thames, during the late war, were prepared, by it, for the perpetration of every crime, as soon as they were set at liberty from their confinement.

I proceed,

II. To shew, that public punishments, so far from preventing crimes by terror they excite in the minds of spectators, are directly calculated to produce them. . . .

The history of public punishments, in every age and country, is full of facts, which support every principle that has been advanced. —What has been the operation of the seventy thousand executions, that have taken place in Great-Britain from the year 1688, to the present day, upon the morals and manners of the inhabitants of that island? Has not every prison door that has been opened, to conduct criminals to public shame and punishments, unlocked, at the same time, the bars of moral obligation upon the minds of ten times the number of people? How often do we find pockets picked under a gallows, and highway-robberies committed within sight of a gibbet? From whence arose the conspiracies, assassinations, and poisonings, which prevailed in the decline of the Roman empire? Were they not favoured by the public executions of the amphitheatre? It is therefore to the combined operation of indolence, prejudice, ignorance—and the defect of culture of the human heart, alone, that we are to ascribe the continuance of public punishments, after such long and multiplied experience of their inefficacy to reform bad men, or to prevent the commission of crimes.

III. Let it not be supposed, from any thing that has been said, that I wish to abolish punishments. Far from it—I wish only to change the *place* and *manner* of inflicting them, so as to render them effectual for the reformation of criminals, and beneficial to society. Before I propose a plan for this purpose, I beg leave to deliver the following general axioms:

1st, The human mind is disposed to exaggerate every thing that is removed at a distance from it by *time* or *place.*

2dly, It is equally disposed to enquire after, and to magnify such things as are *secret.*

3dly, It always ascribes the extremes in qualities, to things that are *unknown;* and an excess in duration, to *indefinite* time.

4thly, Certain, and *definite evil,* by being long contemplated, ceases to be dreaded or avoided. A soldier soon loses, from habit, the fear of death from a bullet, but retains, in common, with other people, the terror of death from sickness or drowning.

5thly, An attachment to kindred and society is one of the strongest feelings in the human heart. A separation from them, therefore, has ever been considered as one of the severest punishments that can be inflicted upon man.

6thly, Personal liberty is so dear to all men, that the loss of it, for an indefinite time, is a punishment so severe, that death has often been preferred to it.

These axioms being admitted (for they cannot be controverted) I shall proceed next to apply them, by suggesting a plan, for the punishment of crimes, which I flatter myself will answer all the ends that have been proposed by them.

1st, Let a large house, of a construction agreeable to its design, be erected in a remote part of the state. Let the avenue to this house be rendered difficult and gloomy by mountains or morasses. Let its doors be of iron; and let the grating, occasioned by opening and shutting them, be encreased by an echo from a neighbouring mountain, that shall extend and continue a sound that shall deeply pierce the soul. Let a guard constantly attend at a gate that shall lead to this place of punishment, to prevent strangers from entering it. Let all the officers of the house be strictly forbidden ever to discover any signs of mirth, or even levity, in the presence of the criminals. To encrease the horror of this abode of discipline and misery, let it be called by some name that shall import its design.

2dly, Let the various kinds of punishment, that are to be inflicted on crimes, be defined and fixed by law. But let no notice be taken, in the law, of the punishment that awaits any particular crime. By these means we shall prevent the mind from accustoming itself to the view of these punishments, so as to destroy their terror by habit. The indifference and levity with which some men suffer the punishment of hanging, is often occasioned by an insensibility that is contracted by the frequent anticipation of it, or by the appearance of the gallows suggesting the rememberance of scenes of criminal festivity, in which it was the subject of humour or ridicule. Besides, punishments should always be varied in degree, according to the temper of criminals, or the progress of their reformation.

3dly, Let the duration of punishments, for all crimes, be limited, but let this limitation be unknown. I conceive this secret to be of the utmost importance in reforming criminals, and preventing crimes. The imagination, when agitated with uncertainty, will seldom fail of connecting the longest duration of punishment, with the smallest crime. . . .

Chapter VIII

FRUSTRATION IN FOREIGN AFFAIRS

Americans were soon disabused of any hope for a speedy reconciliation with England. That the British were not cordially disposed to their former subjects is understandable in retrospect. Indeed, they pursued a hard line in the restrictive trade measures they adopted against American shipping, in their refusal to give up a whole string of strategic northern and western posts stretching from Lake Champlain all the way west to the vital Straits of Mackinac between Lake Michigan and Lake Huron, in the failure to reach agreement on the northeastern boundary controversy, or to compensate American planters for the thousands of American slaves carried away by British armies. Believing that some agreements could be reached on at least a few of these issues, John Jay, Secretary for Foreign Affairs, dispatched John Adams as Minister to the Court of St. James in 1785. As the instructions below indicate, Jay ordered Adams to maintain a firm position and remind the British of the mutual advantages to be obtained from a settlement of the disputes.

As the first minister from the former British colonies, Adams found himself in a ticklish spot on the occasion of his first confrontation with his erstwhile sovereign. In a letter to Jay, Adams recounted his presentation to George III. Despite the relatively amicable meeting, Adams was not able to resolve any of the issues outstanding between the two nations.

Most inflammatory of all issues of foreign relations during the Confederation was the demand of the United States to have Spain agree on the Mississippi River as the western boundary of the new nation and on the free navigation of that river as laid down in the Treaty of 1783 with Great Britain. To Jay it was a familiar story—during his mission in Spain he had explored the same issues several times in face-to-face encounters with the Conde de Floridablanca, foreign minister to Charles III, and with the Conde's English-speaking deputy, Don Diego de Gardoqui. Now, to settle outstanding differences and arrange a commercial treaty, Spain dispatched to New York the same Gardoqui. He felt quite sure, he confided to his superiors in Madrid, that he could manage Jay, whom he believed to be "a very self-centered man" whose vanity his wife abetted. "This woman, whom he loves blindly," the Spaniard observed, "dominates him and nothing is done without her consent, so that her opinion prevails, though her husband at first may disagree." From this Gardoqui inferred that "a little management in dealing with her and a few timely gifts will secure the friendship of both, because I have reason to believe that they proceed resolved to make a fortune." No comment could prove further off target, for if Jay was vain and Sally liked society, neither was in the least concerned with building a personal fortune.

Gardoqui arrived in New York in July 1785, was received by Congress, and proceeded to occupy the handsomest residence in town, the Archibald Kennedy house at 1 Broadway. Although he gave the Secretary a gift from Charles III of a stallion (which the scrupulous Jay accepted only after securing Congress's permission), Gardoqui made little headway. The Jay-Gardoqui negotiations gave promise of a stalemate, as had the talks in Spain several years earlier. The American West, which had been penetrated during the Revolution by "long hunters" and scouts, was now being inundated by settlers from the eastern states, and even easterners, much as they might have deplored this drain of cheap labor, realized that if the claims of these westerners were abandoned the Confederation might be split apart.

In his negotiations in Spain, Jay had revealed himself as a staunch defender of America's claims to the navigation of the Mississippi to the sea, but he now felt that, in view of Spain's obduracy and America's impotence, the United States could gain nothing by holding out for the impossible but at least might obtain considerable commercial advantages by agreeing to forbear temporarily the use of the Mississippi within exclusively Spanish limits. In the midst of a furious debate in Congress over the proposal, Jay was summoned to appear before that body. At issue, in addition to the navigation of the Mississippi, was the settlement of the disputed boundary between Spanish West

Florida and the American Southwest. On August 3, 1786, he argued in a carefully reasoned speech that it would be better "to yield a few acres than to part in ill-humor." After reviewing the commercial advantages that the proposed treaty held out to America, and they were manifold, Jay came to the heart of the controversy. Although Congress by a slim majority approved Jay's proposal, it was clear that it would be impossible to secure the necessary nine states to ratify the treaty. The issue then remained unsettled until the Washington administration.

Nowhere was the weakness of America more evident in the Confederation period than in its relations with the Barbary states. Once independence had been declared, the American shippers had lost the protection of the British navy in the Mediterranean waters and the rulers of the petty North African states began preying upon American commerce. To prevent such depredations, John Jay believed that after enough humiliations at the hands of the Barbary states the American people might see the necessity of strengthening their own government, while John Adams recommended that large sums of tribute money be paid. This, he felt, was cheaper than war. For the moment Adams' advice prevailed, and at the bargain price of $10,000 the United States bought a treaty with Morocco in 1787.

22.   Great Britain: John Jay's Draft of Proposed Instructions to Minister to London March 7, 1785*

Report of Instructions for the Minister to be sent by the United States to the Court of London

You will in a respectful but firm Manner insist that the United States be put, without further Delay, into Possession of all the Posts and Territories within their Limits, which are now held [against their] by british Garisons. And you will take the earliest opportunity of transmitting the answer you may receive to this Requisition.

[You will [sound] endeavor to make yourself acquainted with the Disposition of the british Cabinet, to join with the United States in proper pacific Measures for inducing Spain to cease opposing the free Navigation of the Mississippi and to that End a Display of the commercial advantages which would flow to them through that Channel, would probably prove a powerful Inducement.]

You will remonstrate against the Infraction of the Treaty of Peace, by the Exportation of Slaves and other american Property, contrary to the Stipulations on that Subject in the [   ] article of it. Upon this Head you will be supplied with various authentic Papers and Documents—particularly the Correspondence between General Washington and others on the one Part, and Sir Guy Carlton on the other.

You will represent to the british Ministry the strong and

---

* The John Jay Papers, Special Collections, Columbia University Libraries.

necessary Tendency of their Restrictions on our Trade, to in-
capacitate our Merchants in a certain Degree, to make Remittances to Their's. [You will so manage your Conferences with
the Minister on the Subject of Commerce, as to discover whether
he is inclined to make a Treaty with us and on what Terms—
taking Care not to enter into any Engagements without the previous approbation of Congress.]

You will represent in strong Terms the Losses which many of
our and also of *their* Merchants will sustain, if the former be
unseasonably and immoderately pressed for the payment of
Debts contracted before the War, [and (if Compliance should
appear probable) you will sollicit the Interposition and Influence
of government to prevent[1] it.] On this Subject you will be
furnished with Papers in which it is amply discussed.

[1] Indecipherable in original draft.

23. Great Britain: John Adams' Presentation to George III, June 2, 1785 *

Bath Hotel, Westminster,
June 2, 1785

Dear Sir,
. . . At one, on Wednesday, the first of June, the master of
ceremonies called at my house and went with me to the Secretary of State's Office, in Cleveland Row, where the Marquis of
Carmarthen received me and . . . invited me to go with him in
his coach to Court. When we arrived in the Anti-Chamber, the

* The John Jay Papers, Special Collections, Columbia University Libraries; *Diplomatic Correspondence of the United States of America, 1783–1789* (Washington, 1833), IV, 198–203.

Oeil de Boeuf, of St. James's, the master of the ceremonies met me and attended me, while the Secretary of State went to take the commands of the King. While I stood in this place, where it seems all Ministers stand upon such occasions, always attended by the master of ceremonies, the room very full of Ministers of State, Bishops, and all other sorts of courtiers, as well as the next room, which is the King's bed-chamber, you may well suppose, I was the focus of all eyes . . . until the Marquis of Carmarthen returned and desired me to go with him to his Majesty. I went with his Lordship through the levee room into the King's closet. The door was shut and I was left with his Majesty and the Secretary of State alone, I made the three reverences, one at the door, another about halfway, and the third before the presence, according to the usage established at this and all the northern Courts of Europe, and then addressed myself to his Majesty in the following words:

"Sir,

"The United States of America have appointed me their Minister Plenipotentiary to your Majesty, and have directed me to deliver to your Majesty this letter, which contains the evidence of it. It is in obedience to their express commands that I have the honor to assure your Majesty of their unanimous disposition and desire to cultivate the most friendly and liberal intercourse between your Majesty's subjects and their citizens, and of their best wishes for your Majesty's health and happiness, and that of your royal family. The appointment of a Minister from the United States to your Majesty's Court, will form an epoch in the history of England and of America. I think myself more fortunate than all my fellow-citizens in having the distinguished honor to be the first to stand in your Majesty's royal presence in a diplomatic character, and shall esteem myself the happiest of men, if I can be instrumental in recommending my country more and more to your Majesty's royal benevolence, and of restoring an entire esteem, confidence and affection, or in better words, the old good nature and the old good humor, between people, who though separated by an ocean, and under different governments, have the same language, a similar religion, and kindred blood.

"I beg your Majesty's permission to add, that although I have some time before been intrusted by my country, it was never in my whole life in a manner so agreeable to myself."

The King listened to every word I said with dignity, but with an apparent emotion. Whether it was the nature of the interview, or whether it was my visible agitation, for I felt more than I did or could express, that touched him, I cannot say; but he was much affected, and answered me with more tremor than I had spoken with, and said:

"Sir,

"The circumstances of thy audience are so extraordinary, the language you have now held is so extremely proper, and the feelings you have discovered so justly adapted to the occasion, that I must say that I not only receive with pleasure the assurance of the friendly dispositions of the United States, but that I am very glad the choice has fallen upon you to be their Minister. I wish you, Sir, to believe, and that it may be understood in America, that I have done nothing in the late contest, but what I thought myself indispensably bound to do, by the duty which I owed to my people. I will be very frank with you. I was the last to consent to the separation; but the separation having been made, and having become inevitable, I have always said, as I say now, that I would be the first to meet the friendship of the United States as an independent power. The moment I see such sentiments and language as yours prevail, and a disposition to give to this country the preference, that moment I shall say, let the circumstances of language, religion and blood, have their natural and full effect."

I dare not say that these were the King's precise words, and it is even possible that I may have in some particular mistaken his meaning, for although his pronunciation is as distinct as I ever heard, he hesitated some time between his periods, and between the members of the same period. He was much affected, and I was not less so, and therefore, I cannot be certain that I was so attentive [but] . . . the foregoing is his Majesty's meaning as I then understood it, and his own words as nearly as I can recollect them. . . .

The conversation with the King, Congress will form their own judgment of. I may expect from it a residence less painful than I once expected, as so marked an attention from the King will silence many grumblers; but we can infer nothing from all this concerning the success of my mission. . . .

With great respect, &c.
JOHN ADAMS

24. Navigation of the Mississippi and Development of the West: John Jay's Speech to Congress on Negotiations with Spain's Minister Diego de Gardoqui, August 6, 1786 *

My attention is chiefly fixed on two obstacles, which at present divide us, viz. the Navigation of the Mississippi, and the territorial limits between them and us.

My Letters written from Spain, when our affairs were the least promising, evince my opinion respecting the Mississippi, and oppose every idea of our relinquishing our right to navigate it. I entertain the same sentiments of that right, and of the importance of retaining it, which I then did.

Mr. Gardoqui strongly insists on our relinquishing it. We have had many Conferences and much reasoning on the subject, not necessary now to detail. His concluding answer to all my Arguments has steadily been, that the King will never yield that point, nor consent to any compromise about it; for that it always has been, and continues to be, one of their Maxims of policy, to exclude all Mankind from their American shores.

I have often reminded him that the adjacent Country was filling fast with people; and that the time must and would come, when they would not submit to seeing a fine river flow before their doors without using it as a high way to the sea for the transportation of their productions; that it would therefore be

* Ford (ed.), *Journals of the Continental Congress,* XXXI, 479–481.

wise to look forward to that event, and take care not to sow in
the treaty any seeds of future discord. He said that the time
alluded to was far distant; and that treaties were not to provide
for contingencies so remote and future. For his part he considered the rapid settlement of that Country as injurious to the
States, and that they would find it necessary to check it. Many
fruitless Arguments passed between us; and tho' he would admit
that the only way to make treaties and friendship permanent,
was for neither party to leave the other any thing to complain
of; yet he would still insist, that the Mississippi must be shut
against us. The truth is, that Courts never admit the force of any
reasoning or Arguments but such as apply in their favor; and it
is equally true, that even if our right to that Navigation, or to
any thing else, was expressly declared in Holy Writ, we should
be able to provide for the enjoyment of it no otherwise than by
being in capacity to repel force by force.

Circumstanced as we are, I think it would be expedient to
agree that the treaty should be limited to twenty five or thirty
years, and that one of the Articles should stipulate that the
United States would forbear to use the Navigation of that River
below their territories to the Ocean. Thus the duration of the
treaty and of the forbearance in question would be limited to
the same period.

Whether Mr. Gardoqui would be content with such an Article,
I cannot determine, my instructions restraining me from even
sounding him respecting it. I nevertheless think the experiment
worth trying for several reasons:

1. Because unless that matter can in some way or other be
settled, the treaty, however advantageous, will not be concluded.

2. As that Navigation is not *at present* important, nor will
probably become much so in less than twenty five or thirty years,
a forbearance to use it while we do not *want it,* is no great sacrifice.

3. Spain now excludes us from that Navigation, and with a
strong hand holds it against us. She will not yield it peaceably,
and therefore we can only acquire it by *War.* Now as we are not
prepared for a War with any power; as many of the States
would be little inclined to a War with Spain for that object at
this day; and as such a War would for those and a variety of ob-

vious reasons be inexpedient, it follows, that Spain will, for a long space of time yet to come, exclude us from that Navigation. Why therefore should we not (for a valuable Consideration too) consent to forbear to use what we know is not in our power to use.

4. If Spain and the United States should part on this point, what are the latter to do? Will it after that be consistent with their dignity to permit Spain forcibly to exclude them from a right, which, at the expense of a beneficial treaty, they have asserted? They will find themselves obliged either to do this, and be humiliated, or they must attack Spain. Are they ripe and prepared for this? I wish I could say they are.

It is possible that such an Article, if agreed to, might lessen one of the arguments urged to enhance the value of Western lands; but would not the Spaniards continuing by force to exclude us from the navigation soon have the same effect? In either case that Argument must lose some of its force; but in the one case America would also lose some of its dignity. It can be no question therefore which of the two cases would be least desirable.

If such a compromise should be attempted, and not succeed, we shall lose nothing by it; for they who take a lease admit the right of the Lessor.

25.   Barbary States: John Jay to the President of Congress, Richard Henry Lee, October 13, 1785*

Office for Foreign Affairs
13th October 1785

Sir

. . . This War does not strike me as a great Evil. The more we are treated ill abroad, the more we shall unite and consolidate at Home. Besides, as it may become a Nursery for Seamen, and lay the Foundation for a respectable Navy, it may eventually prove more beneficial than otherwise. Portugal will doubtless unite with us in it, and that Circumstance may dispose that Kingdom to extend commercial Favors to us farther, than they might consent to do, if uninfluenced by such Inducements. For my Part I think it may be demonstrated, that while we bend our Attention to the Sea, every *naval* War however long, which does not do us essential Injury, will do us essential Good. . . .

* The John Jay Papers, Special Collections, Columbia University Libraries.

26. Barbary States: John Adams to John Jay, February 17 and 22, 1786*

Grosvenor Square
17 February 1786

Sir,—At a late levee, the King, in conversation with one of the foreign ministers, was pleased to say "that the Tripoline ambassador refused to confer with his ministers, and insisted on an audience; but that nothing had been said at it more than that Tripoli and England were at peace, and desirous to continue so." His Majesty added, "all he wants is a present, and his expenses borne to Vienna and Denmark."

If nothing more was said at the audience, there are not wanting persons in England who will find means to stimulate this African to stir up his countrymen against American vessels. It may reasonably be suspected that his present visit is chiefly with a view to the United States, to draw them into a treaty of peace, which implies tribute, or at least presents; or to obtain aids from England to carry on a war against us. Feeling his appearance here to be ominous, like that of other irregular bodies, which, "from their horrid hair, shake pestilence and war," I thought, at first, to avoid him; but, finding that all the other foreign ministers had made their visits, and that he would take amiss a longer inattention, it was judged necessary to call at his door, for the form; but, when the attempt was made, which was last evening, so late that there was no suspicion of his being visible, the ambassador was announced at home, and ready to

* C. F. Adams, *Works of John Adams,* 10 vols. (Boston, 1851–66), III, 372–373, 378–379.

receive the visitant. It would scarcely be reconcilable to the dignity of congress to read a detail of the ceremonies which attended the conference; it would be more proper to write them to harlequin, for the amusement of the gay at the New York theatre.

It is sufficient to say, that his Excellency made many inquiries concerning America, the climate, soil, heat, cold, &c., and observed, "it is a very great country, but *Tripoli is at war with it.*" In return, it was asked how there could be war between two nations, when there had been no hostility, injury, insult, or provocation on either side. His Excellency replied, that Turkey, Tripoli, Tunis, Algiers, and Morocco were the sovereigns of the Mediterranean; and that no nation could navigate that sea without a treaty of peace with them; that America must make such treaties with Tripoli first, then with Constantinople, then with Algiers and Morocco, as France, England, and all the other powers of Europe had done.

22 February 1786

When he began to explain himself concerning his demands, he said, "they would be different, according to the duration of the treaty; if that were perpetual, they would be greater; if for a term of years, less. His advice was, that it should be perpetual. Once signed by the bashaw, dey, and other officers, it would be indissoluble, and binding forever upon all their successors. But, if a temporary treaty were made, it might be difficult and expensive to revive it; for a perpetual treaty, such as they had now with Spain, a sum of thirty thousand guineas must be paid upon the delivery of the articles signed by the dey and other officers. If it were agreed to, he would send his secretary by land to Marseilles, and from thence by water to Tripoli, who should bring it back by the same route, signed by the dey, &c. He had proposed so small a sum in consideration of the circumstances, but declared it was not half of what had been lately paid them by Spain. If we chose to treat upon a different plan, he would make a treaty perpetual, upon the payment of twelve thousand five hundred guineas for the first year, and three thousand guineas annually, until the thirty thousand guineas were paid." It was observed that these were large sums, and vastly beyond expectation. But his Excellency answered, that they never made a treaty for less.

Upon the arrival of a prize, the dey and the other officers were entitled by law to large shares, by which they might make greater profits than these sums amounted to, and they never would give up this advantage for less.

He was told, that, although there was a full power to treat, the American ministers were limited to a much smaller sum; so that it would be impossible to do anything until we could write to congress and know their pleasure. Colonel Smith was present at this, as he had been at the last conference, and agreed to go to Paris to communicate all to Mr. Jefferson, and persuade him to come here, that we may join in further conferences, and transmit the result to congress. The ambassador believed that Tunis and Morocco would treat upon the same terms, but would not answer for Algiers; they would demand more. When Mr. Jefferson arrives, we shall insist upon knowing the ultimatum, and transmit it to congress.

Congress will perceive that one hundred and twenty thousand guineas will be indispensable to conclude with the four powers at this rate, besides a present to the ambassadors and other incidental charges; besides this, a present of five hundred guineas is made upon the arrival of a consul in each State. No man wishes more fervently that the expense could be less; but the fact cannot be altered; and the truth ought not to be concealed.

It may be reasonably concluded that this great affair cannot be finished for much less than two hundred thousand pounds sterling. There is no place in Europe or America where congress can obtain such a sum but in Holland; perhaps a loan for two millions of guilders might be filled in Amsterdam upon the terms of the last. If it is not done, this war will cost us more millions of sterling money in a short time, besides the miserable depression of the reputation of the United States, the cruel embarrassment of all our commerce, and the intolerable burthen of insurance, added to the cries of our countrymen in captivity.

Chapter IX

THE LAND QUESTION

One of the most vexing problems facing the new Confederation was the ownership of western lands. During the Revolution a number of states, on the basis of old colonial charters, resumed their often conflicting titles to these lands. However, Maryland, which had no western claims, refused to sign the Articles of Confederation unless these areas were ceded to Congress, to be parceled out into "free, convenient, and independent governments." In October 1780, Congress recommended that all states having titles to western lands surrender them to the central government. This resolution, followed by the cession of claims by New York and Connecticut, eventually influenced Virginia, which had the largest claims, to yield her western territory.

In 1784, a plan was drawn up by Thomas Jefferson for the organization of government in the western territories. Following its adoption, an ordinance was then drafted for the sale and survey of these lands. This ordinance, also largely the work of Jefferson, provided that the new lands should be divided into townships each containing thirty-six square miles. One lot in each township was to be set aside for public schools. The Land Ordinance of 1785 helped lay the foundations for the public land system which emerged in the United States.

Although Jefferson's plan of government for the western territory established certain general principles, it did not set up a full administrative structure. At the urging of western settlers, land companies, and a report by a Congressional committee, a new ordinance was adopted which stands as the most notable achievement of the Congress of the Confederation. The Northwest Ordinance provided for a governor, secretary, and three judges appointed by Congress and established the mechanisms whereby territories could achieve statehood, outlawed slavery in the territories north of the Ohio, and established the novel anticolonial principle of admitting new states on a basis of equality with the old.

117

27.   Virginia's Cession of Western Claims to the United States, December 20, 1783 *

SECTION 1

Whereas the Congress of the United States did, by their act of the 6th day of September, in the year 1780, recommend to the several States in the Union, having claims to waste and unappropriated lands in the western country, a liberal cession to the United States of a portion of their respective claims for the common benefit of the union:

SECTION 2

And whereas this commonwealth did, on the 2d day of January, in the year 1781, yield to the Congress of the United States, for the benefit of the said States, all right, title, and claim which the said commonwealth had to the territory northwest of the river Ohio, subject to the conditions annexed to the said act of cession:

SECTION 3

And whereas the United States in Congress assembled have, by their act of the 13th of September last, stipulated the terms on which they agreed to accept the cession of this State, should the legislature approve thereof, which terms, although they do not come up to the proposition of this commonwealth, are conceived, on the whole, to approach so nearly to them as to induce this State to accept thereof, in full confidence that Congress will, in

* F. N. Thorpe (ed.), *Federal and State Constitutions,* II, 955–956.

justice to this State for the liberal cession she hath made, earnestly press upon the other States claiming large tracts of waste and uncultivated territory the propriety of making cessions equally liberal for the common benefit and support of the Union:

Be it enacted by the general assembly, That it shall and may be lawful for the delegates of this State to the Congress of the United States, . . . to . . . make over unto the United States, in Congress assembled, for the benefit of the said States, all right, title, and claim, as well of soil as jurisdiction, which this commonwealth hath to the territory or tract of country within the limits of the Virginia charter, situate, lying, and being to the northwest of the river Ohio, subject to the terms and conditions contained in the before-recited act of Congress of the 13th day of September last, that is to say: Upon condition that the territory so ceded shall be laid out and formed into States, containing a suitable extent of territory, not less than one hundred nor more than one hundred and fifty miles square, or as near thereto as circumstances will admit; and the States so formed shall be distinct republican States, and admitted members of the Federal Union, having the same rights of sovereignty, freedom, and independence as the other States; that the necessary and reasonable expences incurred by this State in subduing any British posts, or in maintaining forts or garrisons within and for the defence, or in acquiring any part of the territory so ceded or relinquished, shall be fully reimbursed by the United States; and that one commissioner shall be appointed by Congress, one by this commonwealth and another by those two commissioners, who, or a majority of them, shall be authorized and empowered to adjust and liquidate the account of the necessary and reasonable expenses incurred by the State, which they shall judge to be comprised within the intent and meaning of the act of Congress of the 10th of October, 1780, respecting such expenses. That of the French and Canadian inhabitants, and other settlers of the Kaskaskies, Saint Vincents and the neighboring villages, who have professed themselves citizens of Virginia, shall have their possessions and titles confirmed to them, and be protected in the enjoyment of their rights and liberties. That a quantity, not exceeding one hundred and fifty thousand acres, of land, promised by this State, shall be allowed and granted to the then Colonel, now

General, George Rogers Clark, and to the officers and soldiers of his regiment who marched with him when the posts of Kaskaskies and Saint Vincents were reduced, and to the officers and soldiers that have been since incorporated into the said regiment, to be laid off in one tract, the length of which not to exceed double the breadth, in such place on the northwest side of the Ohio as a majority of the officers shall choose, and to be afterwards divided among the said officers and soldiers in due proportion according to the law of Virginia. That in case the quantity of good lands on the southeast side of the Ohio, upon the waters of Cumberland River, and between Green River and Tennessee River, which have been reserved by law for the Virginia troops upon continental establishment, should, from the North Carolina line bearing in further upon the Cumberland lands than was expected, prove insufficient for their legal bounties, the deficiency should be made up to the said troops in good lands, to be laid off between the rivers Scioto and Little Miami, on the northwest side of the river Ohio, in such proportions as have been engaged to them by the laws of Virginia. That all the lands within the territory so ceded to the United States, and not reserved for or appropriated to any of the before-mentioned purposes, or disposed of in bounties to the officers and soldiers of the American Army, shall be considered as a common fund for the use and benefit of such of the United States as have become, or shall become members of the confederation or federal alliance of the said States, Virginia inclusive, according to their usual respective proportions in the general charge and expenditure, and shall be faithfully and *bona fide* disposed of for that purpose, and for no other use or purpose whatsoever: *Provided,* That the trust hereby reposed in the delegates of this State shall not be executed unless three of them, at least, are present in Congress.

28.   Land Ordinance of 1785, May 20, 1785*

*An Ordinance for ascertaining the mode
of disposing of Lands in the Western
Territory*

BE it ordained by the United States in Congress assembled,
that the territory ceded by individual States to the United States,
which has been purchased of the Indian inhabitants, shall be disposed of in the following manner:

A surveyor from each state shall be appointed by Congress or
a Committee of the States, who shall take an oath for the faithful discharge of his duty, before the Geographer of the United
States. . . .

The Surveyors, as they are respectively qualified, shall proceed
to divide the said territory into townships of six miles square, by
lines running due north and south, and others crossing these at
right angles, as near as may be, unless where the boundaries of
the late Indian purchases may render the same impracticable, . . .

The first line, running due north and south as aforesaid, shall
begin on the river Ohio, at a point that shall be found to be due
north from the western termination of a line, which has been
run as the southern boundary of the State of Pennsylvania; and
the first line, running east and west, shall begin at the same
point, and shall extend throughout the whole territory. Provided,

* W. C. Ford, *et al.* (eds.), *Journals of the Continental Congress,*
XXVIII, 375 *et seq.*

that nothing herein shall be construed, as fixing the western boundary of the State of Pennsylvania. The geographer shall designate the townships, or fractional parts of townships, by numbers progressively from south to north; always beginning each range with No. 1; and the ranges shall be distinguished by their progressive numbers to the westward. The first range, extending from the Ohio to the lake Erie, being marked No. 1. The Geographer shall personally attend to the running of the first east and west line; and shall take the latitude of the extremes of the first north and south line, and of the mouths of the principal rivers.

The lines shall be measured with a chain; shall be plainly marked by chaps on the trees, and exactly described on a plat; whereon shall be noted by the surveyor, at their proper distances, all mines, salt-springs, salt-licks and mill-seats, that shall come to his knowledge, and all water-courses, mountains and other remarkable and permanent things, over and near which such lines shall pass, and also the quality of the lands.

The plats of the townships respectively, shall be marked by subdivisions into lots of one mile square, or 640 acres, in the same direction as the external lines, and numbered from 1 to 36; always beginning the succeeding range of the lots with the number next to that with which the preceding one concluded. . . .

. . . And the geographer shall make . . . returns, from time to time, of every seven ranges as they may be surveyed. The Secretary of War shall have the recourse thereto, and shall take by lot therefrom, a number of townships . . . as will be equal to one seventh part of the whole of such seven ranges, . . . for the use of the late Continental army. . . .

The board of treasury shall transmit a copy of the original plats, previously noting thereon the townships and fractional parts of townships, which shall have fallen to the several states, by the distribution aforesaid, to the commissioners of the loan-office of the several states, who, after giving notice . . . shall proceed to sell the townships or fractional parts of townships, at public vendue, in the following manner, viz.: The township or fractional part of a township No. 1, in the first range, shall be sold entire; and No. 2, in the same range, by lots; and thus in alternate order through the whole of the first range . . . provided, that none of the lands, within the said territory, be sold under the price of one dollar the acre, to be paid in specie, or loan-office certificates, reduced to species value, by the scale of depreciation, or certificates of liquidated debts of the United States, including interest, besides the expense of the survey and other charges thereon, which are hereby rated at thirty six dollars the township, . . . on failure of which payment, the said lands shall again be offered for sale.

There shall be reserved for the United States out of every township the four lots, being numbered 8, 11, 26, 29, and out of every fractional part of a township, so many lots of the same numbers as shall be found thereon, for future sale. There shall be reserved the lot No. 16, of every township, for the maintenance of public schools within the said township; also one-third part of all gold, silver, lead and copper mines, to be sold, or otherwise disposed of as Congress shall hereafter direct. . . .

And Whereas Congress . . . stipulated grants of land to certain officers and soldiers of the late Continental army . . . for complying with such engagements, Be it ordained, That the secretary of war . . . determine who are the objects of the above resolutions and engagements . . . and cause the townships, or fractional parts of townships, hereinbefore reserved for the use of the late Continental army, to be drawn for in such manner as he shall deem expedient. . . .

29.   Northwest Ordinance, July 13, 1787 *

*An Ordinance for the government of the
Territory of the United States northwest
of the River Ohio*

Be it ordained by the United States in Congress assembled,
That the said territory, for the purposes of temporary government, be one district, subject, however, to be divided into two
districts, as future circumstances may, in the opinion of Congress, make it expedient.

Be it ordained by the authority aforesaid, That the estates,
both of resident and nonresident proprietors in the said territory,
dying intestate, shall descend to, and be distributed among their
children, and the descendants of a deceased child, in equal parts;
the descendants of a deceased child or grandchild to take the
share of their desceased parent in equal parts among them: And
where there shall be no children or descendants, then in equal
parts to the next of kin in equal degree; and among collaterals,
the children of a deceased brother or sister of the intestate shall
have, in equal parts among them, their deceased parents' share;
and there shall in no case be a distinction between kindred of
the whole and half-blood; saving, in all cases, to the widow of
the intestate her third part of the real estate for life, and one-
third part of the personal estate; and this law relative to descents
and dower, shall remain in full force until altered by the legislature of the district. And until the governor and judges shall adopt

* F. N. Thorpe (ed.), *Federal and State Constitutions*, II, 957 *et seq.*

laws as hereinafter mentioned, estates in the said territory may be devised or bequeathed by wills in writing, signed and sealed by him or her in whom the estate may be (being of full age), and attested by three witnesses; and real estates may be conveyed by lease and release, or bargain and sale, signed sealed and delivered by the person, being of full age, in whom the estate may be, and attested by two witnesses, provided such wills be duly proved, and such conveyances be acknowledged, or the execution thereof duly proved, and be recorded within one year after proper magistrates, courts, and registers shall be appointed for that purpose; and personal property may be transferred by delivery; saving, however to the French and Canadian inhabitants, and other settlers of the Kaskaskies, St. Vincents and the neighboring villages who have heretofore professed themselves citizens of Virginia, their laws and customs now in force among them, relative to the descent and conveyance, of property.

Be it ordained by the authority aforesaid, That there shall be appointed from time to time by Congress, a governor, whose commission shall continue in force for the term of three years, unless sooner revoked by Congress; he shall reside in the district, and have a freehold estate therein in 1,000 acres of land, while in the exercise of his office.

There shall be appointed from time to time by Congress, a secretary, whose commission shall continue in force for four years unless sooner revoked; he shall reside in the district, and have a freehold estate therein in 500 acres of land, while in the exercise of his office. It shall be his duty to keep and preserve the acts and laws passed by the legislature, and the public records of the district, and the proceedings of the governor in his executive department, and transmit authentic copies of such acts and proceedings, every six months, to the Secretary of Congress: There shall also be appointed a court to consist of three judges, any two of whom to form a court, who shall have a common law jurisdiction, and reside in the district, and have each therein a free-hold estate in 500 acres of land while in the exercise of their offices; and their commissions shall continue in force during good behavior.

The governor and judges, or a majority of them, shall adopt and publish in the district such laws of the original States, criminal and civil, as may be necessary and best suited to the circumstances of the district, and report them to Congress from time to time: which laws shall be in force in the district until the organization of the General Assembly therein, unless disapproved of by Congress; but afterwards the Legislature shall have authority to alter them as they shall think fit.

The governor, for the time being, shall be commander-in-chief of the militia, appoint and commission all officers in the same below the rank of general officers; all general officers shall be appointed and commissioned by Congress.

Previous to the organization of the general assembly, the governor shall appoint such magistrates and other civil officers in each county or township, as he shall find necessary for the preservation of the peace and good order in the same: After the general assembly shall be organized, the powers and duties of the magistrates and other civil officers shall be regulated and defined by the said assembly; but all magistrates and other civil officers not herein otherwise directed, shall, during the continuance of this temporary government, be appointed by the governor.

For the prevention of crimes and injuries, the laws to be adopted or made shall have force in all parts of the district, and for the execution of process, criminal and civil, the governor shall make proper divisions thereof; and he shall proceed from time to time as circumstances may require, to lay out the parts of the district in which the Indian titles shall have been extinguished, into counties and townships, subject however to such alterations as may thereafter be made by the legislature.

So soon as there shall be five thousand free male inhabitants of full age in the district, upon giving proof thereof to the governor, they shall receive authority, with time and place, to elect representatives from their counties or townships to represent them in the general assembly: *Provided,* That, for every five hundred free male inhabitants, there shall be one representative, and so on progressively with the number of free male inhabitants shall the right of representation increase, until the number of representatives shall amount to twenty-five; after which, the number and proportion of representatives shall be regulated by the legislature: *Provided,* That no person be eligible or qualified to act as a representative unless he shall have been a citizen of one of the United States three years, and be a resident in the district, or unless he shall have resided in the district three years; and, in either case, shall likewise hold in his own right, in fee simple, two hundred acres of land within the same: *Provided, also,* That a freehold in fifty acres of land in the district, having been a citizen of one of the states, and being resident in the district, or the like freehold and two years residence in the district, shall be necessary to qualify a man as an elector of a representative.

The representatives thus elected, shall serve for the term of two years; and, in case of the death of a representative, or removal from office, the governor shall issue a writ to the county or township for which he was a member, to elect another in his stead, to serve for the residue of the term.

The general assembly or legislature shall consist of the governor, legislative council, and a house of representatives. The Legislative Council shall consist of five members, to continue in office five years, unless sooner removed by Congress; any three of whom to be a quorum: and the members of the Council shall be nominated and appointed in the following manner, to wit: As soon as representatives shall be elected, the Governor shall appoint a time and place for them to meet together; and, when met, they shall nominate ten persons, residents in the district, and each possessed of a freehold in five hundred acres of land, and return their names to Congress; five of whom Congress shall appoint and commission to serve as aforesaid; and, whenever a vacancy shall happen in the council, by death or removal from office, the house of representatives shall nominate two persons, qualified as aforesaid, for each vacancy, and return their names to Congress; one of whom Congress shall appoint and commission for the residue of the term. And every five years, four months at least before the expiration of the time of service of the members of council, the said house shall nominate ten persons, qualified as aforesaid, and return their names to Congress; five of whom Congress shall appoint and commission to serve as members of the council five years, unless sooner removed. And the governor, legislative council, and house of representatives, shall have authority to make laws in all cases, for the good government of the district, not repugnant to the principles and articles in this ordinance established and declared. And all bills, having passed by a majority in the house, and by a majority in the council, shall be referred to the governor for his assent; but no bill, or legislative act whatever, shall be of any force without his assent. The governor shall have power to convene, prorogue, and dissolve the general assembly, when, in his opinion, it shall be expedient.

The governor, judges, legislative council, secretary, and such other officers as Congress shall appoint in the district, shall take an oath or affirmation of fidelity and of office; the governor before the president of congress, and all other officers before the Governor. As soon as a legislature shall be formed in the district, the council and house assembled in one room, shall have authority, by joint ballot, to elect a delegate to Congress, who shall have a seat in Congress, with a right of debating but not of voting during this temporary government.

And, for extending the fundamental principles of civil and religious liberty, which form the basis whereon these republics, their laws and constitutions are erected; to fix and establish those principles as the basis of all laws, constitutions, and governments, which forever hereafter shall be formed in the said territory: to provide also for the establishment of States, and permanent government therein, and for their admission to a share in the federal councils on an equal footing with the original States, at as early periods as may be consistent with the general interest:

It is hereby ordained and declared by the authority aforesaid, That the following articles shall be considered as articles of compact between the original States and the people and States in the said territory and forever remain unalterable, unless by common consent, to wit:

ART. 1

No person, demeaning himself in a peaceable and orderly manner, shall ever be molested on account of his mode of worship or religious sentiments, in the said territory.

ART. 2

The inhabitants of the said territory shall always be entitled to the benefits of the writ of *habeas corpus,* and of the trial by jury; of a proportionate representation of the people in the legislature; and of judicial proceedings according to the course of the common law. All persons shall be bailable, unless for capital offences, where the proof shall be evident or the presumption great. All fines shall be moderate; and no cruel or unusual punishments shall be inflicted. No man shall be deprived of his liberty or property, but by the judgment of his peers or the law of the land; and, should the public exigencies make it necessary, for the common preservation, to take any person's property, or to demand his particular services, full compensation shall be made for the same. And, in the just preservation of rights and property, it is understood and declared, that no law ought ever to be made, or have force in the said territory, that shall, in any manner whatever, interfere with or affect private contracts or engagements, *bona fide,* and without fraud, previously formed.

ART. 3

Religion, morality, and knowledge, being necessary to good government and the happiness of mankind, schools and the means of education shall forever be encouraged. The utmost good faith shall always be observed towards the Indians; their lands and property shall never be taken from them without their consent; and, in their property, rights, and liberty, they shall never be invaded or disturbed, unless in just and lawful wars authorized by Congress; but laws founded in justice and humanity, shall from time to time be made for preventing wrongs being done to them, and for preserving peace and friendship with them.

ART. 4

The said territory, and the States which may be formed therein, shall forever remain a part of this Confederacy of the United States of America, subject to the Articles of Confederation, and to such alterations therein as shall be constitutionally made; and to all the acts and ordinances of the United States in Congress assembled, conformable thereto. The inhabitants and settlers in the said territory shall be subject to pay a part of the federal debts contracted or to be contracted, and a proportional part of the expenses of government, to be apportioned on them by

Congress according to the same common rule and measure by which apportionments thereof shall be made on the other States; and the taxes for paying their proportion shall be laid and levied by the authority and direction of the legislatures of the district or districts, or new States, as in the original States, within the time agreed upon by the United States in Congress assembled. The legislatures of those districts or new States, shall never interfere with the primary disposal of the soil by the United States in Congress assembled, nor with any regulations Congress may find necessary for securing the title in such soil to the *bona fide* purchasers. No tax shall be imposed on lands the property of the United States; and, in no case, shall non-resident proprietors be taxed higher than residents. The navigable waters leading into the Mississippi and St. Lawrence, and the carrying places between the same, shall be common highways and forever free, as well to the inhabitants of the said territory as to the citizens of the United States, and those of any other States that may be admitted into the confederacy, without any tax, impost, or duty therefor.

ART. 5

There shall be formed in the said territory, not less than three nor more than five States; and the boundaries of the States, as soon as Virginia shall alter her act of cession, and consent to the same, shall become fixed and established as follows, to wit: The western State in the said territory, shall be bounded by the Mississippi, the Ohio, and Wabash Rivers; a direct line drawn from the Wabash and Post Vincents, due North, to the territorial line between the United States and Canada; and, by the said territorial line, to the Lake of the Woods and Mississippi. The middle State shall be bounded by the said direct line, the Wabash from Post Vincents to the Ohio, by the Ohio, by a direct line, drawn due north from the mouth of the Great Miami, to the said territorial line, and by the said territorial line. The eastern State shall be bounded by the last mentioned direct line, the Ohio, Pennsylvania, and the said territorial line: *Provided, however,* and it is further understood and declared, that the boundaries of these three States shall be subject so far to be altered, that, if Congress shall hereafter find it expedient, they shall have authority to form one or two States in that part of the said territory which lies north of an east and west line drawn through the southerly bend or extreme of lake Michigan. And, whenever any of the said States shall have sixty thousand free inhabitants therein, such State shall be admitted, by its delegates, into the Congress of the United States, on an equal footing with the original States in all respects whatever, and shall be at liberty to form a permanent constitution and State government: *Provided,* the constitution and government so to be formed, shall be republican, and in conformity to the principles contained in these articles; and, so far as it can be consistent with the general interest of the confederacy, such admission shall be allowed at an earlier period, and when there may be a less number of free inhabitants in the State than sixty thousand.

Art. 6

There shall be neither slavery nor involuntary servitude in the said territory, otherwise than in the punishment of crimes whereof the party shall have been duly convicted: *Provided, always,* That any person escaping into the same, from whom labor or service is lawfully claimed in any one of the original States, such fugitive may be lawfully reclaimed and conveyed to the person claiming his or her labor or service as aforesaid.

Be it ordained by the authority aforesaid, That the resolutions of the 23rd of April 1784, relative to the subject of this ordinance, be, and the same are hereby repealed and declared null and void.

Chapter X

INTERNAL TENSIONS

One of the greatest shortcomings of the Articles of Confederation was its failure to provide Congress with an adequate permanent revenue. This became abundantly clear as Congress had to default on its mounting war debts. Beginning in 1781 an attempt was made to remedy the situation by granting Congress permission to levy a five percent duty on imports. Twelve of the thirteen states quickly ratified the measure, but one state, Rhode Island, rejected it, fearing an encroachment upon its autonomy. The ability of one state to thwart any decisive actions by the whole (a unanimous vote was needed to approve any changes in the Articles) pointed to another glaring weakness of the Confederation.

Another major shortcoming of the Articles was its failure to provide a uniform and stable currency. As a depression picked up momentum during the mid-1780's, many states began to issue their own paper money. Though the paper quickly depreciated in value to the despair of creditors, debtors clamored for larger and larger emissions, contributing to deepening the financial chaos. This "rage for paper money" and its inherent dangers are aptly described in a letter from James Madison to Thomas Jefferson.

Since Congress lacked effective power to regulate commerce, many states began to introduce their own tariff and tonnage legislation. In some cases this led to commercial war between neighboring states, with some states levying heavy duties upon the products imported from other states. Connecticut taxed goods from Massachusetts, Pennsylvania levied discriminatory duties upon Delaware, while New York did the same to New Jersey. In 1786, when twelve states again agreed to allow Congress to levy customs duties, New Jersey refused to pay its quota unless New York would stop its discriminatory practices. The problem is

133

related by the French Chargé d'Affaires, Chevalier Louis-Guillaume Otto, in a letter to the Comte de Vergennes, in which he also reports the debtor relief legislation in force in New Jersey and modeled upon the current practices of the Carolinas.

30. Rhode Island's Opposition to the Impost: Letter from the Rhode Island Assembly to Congress, November 30, 1782*

A letter, of the 30 November, from the speaker of the lower house of assembly of the State of Rhode Island, being read,

A motion was made by Mr. [David] Howell, seconded by Mr. [Jonathan] Arnold, in the words following:

"Whereas a letter to his Excellency the President of Congress, from the lower house of assembly of the State of Rhode Island and Providence Plantations, hath been this day read in Congress, in the words and figures following, to wit:

East Greenwich, 30th November, 1782.

Sir: In obedience to the direction of the lower house of assembly of this State, I have the honor to enclose to your Excellency their unanimous resolution on the recommendation of Congress, respecting an impost on imported goods, &c. and to state some of the principal reasons which produced that resolution. The recommendation was rejected.

1st. Because it would be unequal in its operation, bearing hardest on the most commercial states, and so would press peculiarly hard upon this State, which draws its chief support from commerce:

* W. C. Ford, *et al.* (eds.), *Journals of the Continental Congress,* XXIII, 788–789.

2dly. Because it proposes to introduce into this and the other states, officers unknown and unaccountable to them, and so is against the constitution of this State: and

3dly. Because, by granting to Congress a power to collect moneys from the commerce of these states, indefinitely as to time and quantity, and for the expenditure of which they are not to be accountable to the states, they would become independent of their constituents; and so the proposed impost is repugnant to the liberty of the United States.

Many more reasons might be offered, and the subject drawn out to a great length, by descending to particulars; but these are sufficient to answer the main design of the house, which is to shew a decent respect to the states which have differed from them in opinion upon this subject.

This State may be justly ranked among the foremost in the common cause, having furnished in support of it as many men, and as much money, in proportion to its abilities, as any State in the union, and much more than most of them, and it is still disposed to continue its exertions; but it will raise and collect its quota of public taxes in such a way as shall be judged most proper.

And it is hoped, that when its resolutions are founded on the great principles of liberty and a general interest, it will not be thought to suspect the public virtue of the present Congress, by withholding from them or their servants, a power of which their successors might make a dangerous use.

With the highest sentiments of respect for your Excellency, and the honorable assembly over which you preside, I am your Excellency's most obedient servant,

WILLIAM BRADFORD, *Speaker*.

31.   Rage for Paper Money: James Madison to Thomas Jefferson, August 12, 1786 *

These fruits of the Revolution do great honour to it. I wish all our proceedings merited the same character. Unhappily, there are but too many belonging to the opposite side of the account. At the head of these is to be put the general rage for paper money. Pennsylvania and North Carolina took the lead in this folly. In the former the sum emitted was not considerable, the funds for sinking it were good, and it was not made a legal tender. It issued into circulation partly by way of loan to individuals on landed security, partly by way of payment to the public creditors. Its present depreciation is about 10 or 12 per cent. In North Carolina the sums issued at different times have been of greater amount, and it has constantly been a tender. It issued partly in payments to military creditors, and, latterly, in purchases of Tobacco on public account. The Agent, I am informed, was authorised to give nearly the double of the current price; and as the paper was a tender, debtors ran to him with their Tobacco, and the creditors paid the expence of the farce. The depreciation is said to be 25 or 30 per cent. in that State. South Carolina was the next in order. Her emission was in the way of loans to individuals, and is not a legal tender. But land is there made a tender in case of suits, which shuts the Courts of Justice, and is, perhaps, as great an evil. The friends of the emission say that it has not yet depreciated, but they admit that the

* G. Hunt (ed.), *Writings of James Madison,* 9 vols. (New York, 1900–1910), II, 259–262.

price of commodities has risen, which is evidently the form in which depreciation will first shew itself.

New Jersey has just issued £30,000 (dollar at 7s. 6d.) in loans to her citizens. It is a legal tender. An addition of £100,-000 is shortly to follow on the same principles. The terror of popular associations stifles, as yet, an overt discrimination between it and specie; but as this does not operate in Philadelphia and New York, where all the trade of New Jersey is carried on, its depreciation has already commenced in those places, and must soon communicate itself to New Jersey. New York is striking £200,000 (dollar at 8s.) on the plan of loans to her citizens. It is made a legal tender in case of suits only. As it is but just issuing from the press, its depreciation exists only in the foresight of those who reason without prejudice on the subject. In Rhode Island, £100,000 (dollar at 6s.) has lately been issued in loans to individuals. It is not only made a tender, but severe penalties annexed to the least attempt, direct or indirect, to give a preference to specie. Precautions dictated by distrust in the rulers soon produced it in the people. Supplies were withheld from the Market, the Shops were shut, popular meetings ensued, and the State remains in a sort of convulsion.

The Legislature of Massachusetts at their last session rejected a paper emission by a large majority. Connecticut and New Hampshire, also, have as yet forborne, but symptoms of danger, it is said, begin to appear in the latter. The Senate of Maryland has hitherto been a bar to paper in that State. The clamor for it is now universal, and as the periodical election of the Senate happens at this crisis, and the whole body is, unluckily, by their Constitution, to be chosen at once, it is probable that a paper emission will be the result. If, in spite of the zeal exerted against the old Senate, a majority of them should be re-elected, it will require all their firmness to withstand the popular torrent. Of the affairs of Georgia I know as little as of those of Kamskatska.

Whether Virginia is to remain exempt from the epidemic malady will depend on the ensuing Assembly. My hopes rest chiefly on the exertions of Col. Mason, and the failure of the experiments elsewhere. That these must fail is morally certain; for besides the proofs of it already visible in some States, and the intrinsic defect of the paper in all, this fictitious money will rather feed than cure the spirit of extravagance which sends away the coin to pay the unfavorable balance, and will therefore soon be carried to market to buy up coin for that purpose. From that moment depreciation is inevitable. The value of money consists in the uses it will serve. Specie will serve all the uses of paper; paper will not serve one of the essential uses of specie. The paper, therefore, will be less valuable than specie. Among the numerous ills with which this practice is pregnant, one, I find, is, that it is producing the same warfare and retaliation among the States as were produced by the State regulations of commerce. Massachusetts and Connecticut have passed laws enabling their citizens who are debtors to citizens of States having paper money, to pay their debts in the same manner as their citizens who are creditors to citizens of the latter States are liable to be paid their debts.

32. New York vs. New Jersey Commercial Controversy: French Chargé d'Affaires Chevalier Louis-Guillaume Otto to Foreign Minister Comte de Vergennes, March 17, 1786 *

While the different states are active in granting the requisition of last September, and also a duty of five per cent on all importations, congress has been informed that New Jersey had suddenly recalled the powers which it had already given, and that it had refused to levy its contingent for the expenses of the confederation. The motive for this revolting conduct was jealousy,

* Correspondance Politique: États-Unis, Ministère des Affaires Étrangères, Paris; translated in George Bancroft, *History of the Formation of the Constitution of the United States of America,* 3rd ed., 2 vols. (New York, 1883), I, 485–488.

on the part of New Jersey, of New York, which by its position enjoys an advantage in carrying on a great part of its commerce, and which, by means of its customs duties, levies a sort of impost upon New Jersey and Connecticut. New York, not having acceded to the resolutions of congress, derives a great advantage from its customs, and obliges its neighbors, which have no large commercial towns, to pay a part of the expenses of its government. Congress on this occasion thought proper to take a step which could only be taken in the most urgent circumstances. It appointed a deputation composed of three of its members to represent to the legislature of New Jersey, in the most solemn maner, the deplorable consequences of its action. This embassy was received with the respect due to the members of the sovereign body. The legislature granted them a public audience. Mr. Pinckney, delegate from South Carolina, the head of the deputation, made a speech. He began by setting forth the means, the views, and the resources of the confederation. He made it evident that the individual states ought to be impressed with the idea of their weakness as separate governments; that their prosperity and their political existence depended wholly on their union; that it was with this salutary view that the confederation had been formed; that congress alone was the centre of all the powers which are the basis of their national strength; that it alone had the right to make war or peace, to conclude treaties or alliances, to equip fleets, to raise armies, to make laws in the name and on the account of the United States, and to fix the contingent of each member of the union for the common expenses of the government; but that these contingents had been hitherto insufficient, and that the project of a general impost throughout the United States was the only effective means that congress had been able to devise to meet its numerous engagements; that if New Jersey had manifested its resentment against the state of New York by laying extraordinary duties upon all goods imported from that state, and by opening a free port even opposite the city of New York, all the members of the union would have applauded. Its present conduct in refusing the constitutional demands of congress, and in plunging all its companion states into an abyss from which they could only emerge with great difficulty, would divert the attention of the confederation, and would cause the criminal obstinacy of New York to be forgotten. For what inconsistency would it not be in congress, to be severe against that state, while it should allow another member of the union to refuse with impunity its consent to federal measures? Mr. Pinckney added to these arguments very long details on the finances of the United States and upon the necessity of sustaining the confederation. Another deputy,[1] more animated than he, and indignant that the less important states should continue to oppose national measures, exclaimed, among other things, "What is your object in hastening the dissolution of a confederation which has cost us so dear? That compact was the result of necessity; but do you suppose that in a new system of government you would be allowed the importance that you have had hitherto? Do you think that Virginia, South Carolina, Pennsylvania, and Massachusetts would be willing to stand on an equal footing with the handful of citizens which inhabit your state? Although greatly inferior to those powerful republics, you have had an equal part in the deliberations of congress; but in a new confederation you will be put in your proper place." These vigorous words produced a good effect. The assembly of New Jersey has just repealed its resolutions; and, to force New York to submit to the wish of congress, it establishes a free port at Paulus Hook, lying to the west of the mouth of the North river, opposite New York. This port can do great damage to the commerce of that state, and it is hoped that a measure so decisive, the appeals of all the members of the union, and the activity of congress, seated in that city, will finally prevail in changing its system. All the other states have been struck with the deplorable situation of the finances. Maryland, Georgia, and Rhode Island, which had not as yet granted the impost of five per cent, have recently assented to it unanimously. As to New Jersey, it has merely recalled the resolution which it had taken against the impost, but it has not yet done anything toward its adoption, and its legislature dissolved without adjournment. The mania for paper money, which prevails more than ever in America, has caused great divisions in that state. The governor, who opposed it, was hung in effigy, and it is believed that all the members who were unfavorable to this measure will not be re-elected at the next elections.

[1] William Grayson.

Even this method of paying their debts, however dishonest, does not satisfy the people of New Jersey; they desire to pass a law of which the two Carolinas have furnished the first example. By this unjust law, an insolvent debtor has the right of giving up to his creditor any portion whatever of land; *according to the appraisement of his neighbors,* and after this cession of land the creditor has no further means of proceeding against his debtor. The latter is careful to choose the worst of his lands, on which he induces his neighbors, who are themselves debtors and therefore interested in favoring themselves by an exorbitant valuation, to place any price whatever, and after this formality he forces his creditor to accept his land, and even at times to pay him an imagined excess. By this unworthy means a debt of three thousand pounds sterling has often been expunged by land not worth two hundred, and the English merchants have been ruined in Carolina.

Honest people cannot refrain from comparing this conduct with that of the people of Rome; they demanded, at least without subterfuge, and often with arms in their hands, the abolition of debts, while the Americans endeavor to give to the most crying injustice an air of equity, of which no one can be the dupe. They call this law of Carolina the *Barren Land Law,* and their creditors take good care not to press them, fearing to acquire land which they do not want. It is believed that New Jersey will imitate this fine legislation; the paper money which it demands so urgently will, besides, be very favorable to it, and will furnish to the unjust debtor great facilities for discharging his debts legally.

Chapter XI

DETERIORATION AND INSURRECTION

In 1786 economic conditions touched their postwar low, with interior New England hit perhaps the hardest. Farmers found themselves going deeper and deeper into debt. Many were forced to mortgage their lands. Petitions of grievances, especially for closing down the courts and for greater emissions of paper money, were sent to the legislatures. In Massachusetts, when the General Court did not yield to the petitioners' demands, large numbers of men in the western part of the state under the leadership of Daniel Shays, a former army officer, took up arms with the intention of securing their demands by force. Governor Bowdoin, after some delay, called out the state militia to stop the insurrectionists. The meeting of the two forces is described in the following letters from General Shepard to General Lincoln.

Encouraged by the Shaysites, men in other states began to arm themselves to try to secure their demands by force. In New Hampshire, sparked by a rumor that Loyalists were to be returned and that the inhabitants would be taxed to compensate them for their lost estates, a mob of 1,500 men surrounded the meeting house in Exeter where the General Court was in session. Governor Sullivan was forced to send for the militia to prevent the insurrection from getting out of hand. In November of '86, it was necessary to call out the militia in Vermont to quell riots in Windsor and Rutland. Some of the men and issues are illustrated by pertinent excerpts from the Vermont state archives. In a sage observation the French consul in New York, M. de la Forest, commented to the French Minister of Marine that the wisest course for the Massachusetts legislature to pursue would be to satisfy the majority of the community in ending the grievances which triggered Shays' Rebellion. Thus, the democratic process, he perceptively observed, channeled grievances through the election machinery and such dissatisfaction would be reflected in a changing composition of the legislature. That is precisely what happened in Massachusetts, where the Old Guard was swept out of office in the election following Shays' Rebellion and legislation enacted substantially correcting the inequities existing at the time of the disturbances.

That internal conditions in America were seriously deteriorating in 1786 and 1787 was becoming clear to many responsible observers. The weakness of the Confederation and the fear of worse things to come unless decisive measures were taken is explicit in the letters of noted Americans such as John Jay and George Washington, and also in the correspondence of a British consul and the French Chargé stationed in the United States. The last-named reported the dissolution of the Confederation as inevitable.

Less objective were the satiric comments of a group of conservative writers who have come to be known as "The Connecticut Wits," and included Benjamin Trumbull, Lemuel Hopkins, David Humphreys, Joel Barlow, and Timothy Dwight. Shays' Rebellion aroused them to the heights of indignation, and they were completely out of sympathy with the paper money experiments in states like Rhode Island. Their thinly-veiled anti-democratic bias exploded in full fervor in the years following the advent of the French Revolution.

33. Shays' Rebellion: Letters of Generals William Shepard and Benjamin Lincoln to Governor James Bowdoin of Massachusetts January 1787 *

General Shepard to Governor Bowdoin

Springfield
January 26, 1787

The unhappy time is come in which we have been obliged to shed blood. Shays, who was at the head of about twelve hundred men, marched yesterday afternoon about four o'clock, towards the public buildings in battle array. He marched his men in an open column by platoons. I sent several times by one of my aides, and two other gentlemen, Captains Buffington and Woodbridge, to him to know what he was after, or what he wanted. His reply was, he wanted barracks, and barracks he would have and stores. The answer returned was he must purchase them dear, if he had them.

He still proceeded on his march until he approached within two hundred and fifty yards of the arsenal. He then made a halt. I immediately sent Major Lyman, one of my aides, and Capt. Buffington to inform him not to march his troops any nearer the arsenal on his peril, as I was stationed here by order of your Excellency and the Secretary at War, for the defence of the public property; in case he did I should surely fire on him and his men. A Mr. Wheeler, who appeared to be one of Shays' aides, met Mr. Lyman, after he had delivered my orders in the most

* Massachusetts Archives, 190, 317–320.

peremptory manner, and made answer, that that was all he wanted. Mr. Lyman returned with his answer.

Shays immediately put his troops in motion, and marched on rapidly near one hundred yards. I then ordered Major Stephens, who commanded the artillery, to fire upon them. He accordingly did. The two first shots he endeavored to overshoot them, in hopes they would have taken warning without firing among them, but it had no effect on them. Major Stephens then directed his shot through the center of his column. The fourth or fifth shot put their whole column into the utmost confusion. Shays made an attempt to display the column, but in vain. We had one howitz which was loaded with grapeshot, which when fired, gave them great uneasiness.

Had I been disposed to destroy them, I might have charged upon their rear and flanks with my infantry and the two field pieces, and could have killed the greater part of his whole army within twenty-five minutes. There was not a single musket fired on either side. I found three men dead on the spot, and one wounded, who is since dead. One of our artillery men by inattention was badly wounded. Three muskets were taken up with the dead, which were all deeply loaded.

I have received no reinforcement yet, and expect to be attacked this day by their whole force combined.

General Lincoln to Governor Bowdoin

Head Quarters, Springfield
January 28th, 1787

We arrived here yesterday about noon with one regiment from Suffolk, one from Essex, one from Middlesex, and one from Worcester, with three companies of artillery, a corps of horse, and a volunteer corps under the command of Colonel Baldwin; the other company of artillery with the other regiment from Middlesex and another from Worcester which were as a cover to our stores arrived about eight o'clock in the evening. On my arrival, I found that Shays had taken a post at a little village six miles north of this, with the whole force under his immediate command, and that Day had taken post in West Springfield, and that he had fixed a guard at the ferry house on the west side of the river, and that he had a guard at the bridge over Agawam river. By this disposition all communication from the north and west in the usual paths was cut off.

From a consideration of this insult on Government, that by an early move we should instantly convince the insurgents of its ability and determination speedily to disperse them; that we wanted the houses occupied by these men to cover our own troops; that General Patterson was on his march to join us, which to obstruct was an object with them; that a successful movement would give spirits to the troops; that it would be so was reduced to as great a certainty, as can be had in operations of this kind; from these considerations, Sir, with many others, I was induced to order the troops under arms at three o'clock in the afternoon, although the most of them had been so from one in the morning.

We moved about half after three, and crossed the river upon the ice, with the four regiments; four pieces of artillery; the light horse, and the troops of this division, under General Shepard moved up the river on the ice, with an intention to fall in between Shays who was on the east side of the river, and Day on the west, and to prevent a junction as well as to cut off Day's retreat. We supposed that we should hereby encircle him with a force so superior that he would not dare to fire upon us which would effectually prevent bloodshed, *as our troops were enjoined in the most positive manner not to fire without orders*. The moment we showed ourselves upon the river the guard at the ferry house turned out and left the pass open to us. They made a little show of force for a minute or two near the meeting house, and then retired in the utmost confusion and disorder. Our horse met them at the west end of the village, but the insurgents found means by crossing the fields and taking to the woods to escape them; some were taken who are aggravatedly guilty, but not the most so.

The next news we had of them, was by an express from Northampton, that part of them arrived in the south end of their town about eleven o'clock. Shays also in a very precipitate manner left his post a[t] Chickabee, and some time in the night passed through South Hadley, on his way to Amherst.

As soon as our men are refreshed this morning, we shall move northward, leaving General Shepard here as a cover to the magazines; perhaps we may overtake Shays and his party, we shall do it, unless they disperse. If they disperse, I shall cover the troops in some convenient place, and carry on our operations in a very different way.

34. Uprising in New Hampshire, September 23, 1786 *

An Account of the Insurrection in the State of New Hampshire—Written by a Gentlemen who happened to be present

In the beginning of the year 1785, the complaints of the unhappy people, who had contracted debts during the time of the too great plenty of money, induced the legislature to pass an act, making every species of property a tender, at an apprized value. It was soon, however, found from experience, that this answered no other purpose, but to prevent a demand on the part of the creditors and a neglect on the part of the debtors, to discharge their just debts. The scarcity of money still remained a complaint; for as far as goods and real property were substituted as a medium in commerce, so far specie, of course, ceased to circulate; and credit being thus injured, the money-holders turned their keys on that cash which might otherwise have been loaned to the needy.

In August a convention of committees from about thirty towns assembled and agreed upon, and proffered to the General Court a long petition, setting forth their grievances on account of the scarcity of money, and praying for an emission of paper bills of credit, in which there is no single trace of an idea of redemption, or any one attempt to give the currency a foundation, but the whole seems predicated on a supposition that the General Court by a mere act of Legislation by *words* and *signs* could *impress an intrinsic value on paper;* which is as fully absurd as it would be to suppose, that the Legislature had the power of Midas, and could from a single touch, turn stones and sticks into gold: their great object was, however, to have this paper a tender for all debts and taxes, and no plan is hinted, by which the people are to get this money out of the treasury; but it rather seems that they expected the General Court to apportion it among the people at large.

The Legislature formed a plan for the emission of twenty thousand pounds to be let out at four per cent, and land security redeemable at a future period, carrying an interest at six per cent, and to be a tender in taxes for the internal support of the State, and for fees and salaries of the officers of the government. This plan was sent as early as the fourteenth of September, to the several towns, to collect their minds upon the subject.

On the 20 inst. at four of the clock in the afternoon, about 400 men on horse back and on foot, entered the town of Exeter, where the General Court were sitting; about fifty of them, or perhaps more, were armed with muskets, and the others with bludgeons; the principal leader appeared to be one Moses French, a farmer of Hamstead, aided by one Coffin, a Major in the Militia, and two or three others: they affected military parade, and had a drum: after they had halted a while, they sent a paper into the House of Representatives, who were convened in the meeting-house, demanding an answer to their former petition without delay; it was dated on Exeter Plain, and signed Moses French, moderator.

The house appointed a committee of three to be joined by a committee from the senate to take the matter into consideration. This vote the senate unanimously nonconcurred.—Whereupon a conference took place in the meeting-house, between the two branches of the Legislature. The president (General Sullivan) being ex officio, a Senator, opened the matter, by giving publickly, in the hearing of the people, and as many of the mob as chose to attend, the reasons on which the Senate nonconcurred the vote of the House. He first considered the petition, and shewed with great strength of reasoning, and very cooly, the extreme folly, as well as the very great injustice of the prayer of their former petition. And also observed, that even if the measure was just and reasonable, the General Court ought not to pay attention to it, merely from having the voice of thirty towns only, out of two hundred in favour of it. He concluded by saying, that if the voice of the whole State was for the measure, yet the Legislature ought not to comply with it, while they were surrounded by an armed force. To do it would be to betray the rights of the people, which they had all solemnly engaged to support, and that no consideration of personal danger should ever compel him to so flagrant a violation of the constitutional rights of the people, who had placed him in the chair of government.

As soon as this speech was made the mob beat to arms, and surrounded the meeting-house, where the President, the Senate and House remained; those of the mob who had muskets, were ordered to charge with balls, which command they instantly obeyed. The house proceeded to business as usual, without taking any manner of notice of the management at the doors. Centinels were placed at each door, with fixed bayonets, and the whole Legislature were prisoners. After sun-set the president attempted to come out, but was prevented by a firm column. He reasoned very cooly with them on the impropriety and fatal tendency of their conduct, and assured them that the force of the state would support the government: which they took leave to deny with as much confidence as he asserted it. Thus all remained, till the evening was quite dark; the minds of the sober part of the people began to raise at the indignity; while the mob clamoured, some *paper money,* some an equal *distribution of property,* some the *annihilation of debts,* some *release of all taxes,* and all *clamoured against law and government.* A drum was now heard at a distance, and a number of men huzzaing *for government.* The mob appeared frighted, and some of them began to run; the President told them he would prevent bloodshed, and walked through them, and the General Court followed.

On this the insurgents returned to another part of the town, and the Legislature, who had throughout the whole, acted with the most inimitable firmness, and magnanimity, reassumed their business, and requested the President to call forth the power of the state to quell the rebellion. At eleven in the evening he issued his orders, and by sun rise the next morning the militia were marching in, well armed, with military music, and other incidents to military movements. The Major and Brigadier Generals of all the State excepting one whose great remoteness from the scene of action prevented him assembled early in the morning, the gentlemen of the first rank and education emulous to save a government for which they had done, and suffered to much, appeared either on foot or horse in order, and enthusiasm, quite inexpressible by words appeared through the whole. About ten o'clock the President, attended by the general officers, followed by several companies, advanced towards the insurgents who were drawn up at a tavern, in the outer part of the town: There was no conflict; the mob fled, and nothing was to be done but to pick up the prisoners. A number fled and made a stand at a bridge. General Cilly soon came up with them, rushed in and seized their leaders. One of whom ordered them to fire, but government appeared with such force that they dared not to obey. About forty of them were made prisoners and are now in goal to be tried for high treason—the rest are fled to their lurking places, from whence they must be dragged to an ignominious death unless the elemency of government shall pity and save them. By this time there were more than two thousand men in arms, about three hundred of them were horse; all ready to make any risque to preserve legal government, and the due execution of the laws. The sentiments were constantly re-echoed, "How can we live without government, and shall we give ourselves over to a MOB!" If the legislature appeared magnanimous the day before A FREE GOVERNMENT, THE PEOPLE'S GOVERNMENT, shone with a splendor, and glory that never was before equaled. Oh! Massachusetts!—Oh! Massachusetts! Thou who was the chief in thy country! The elder born and most lovely of the daughters of Columbia, how art thou fallen! thy gold is truly become dim, and thy glory departed from thee.

35.   Attempted Insurrection in Vermont, November 1786 to March 1787 *

Attempted Insurrection in Windsor and Rutland Countries

The Windsor paper of November 6, [1786,] mentions, that on the Tuesday, before, being the day assigned by law for the sitting of the court of Common Pleas, for that county, in that town, a Mob, about thirty, under arms, headed by Benjamin Stebbins [farmer, of Barnard,] and Robert Morrison, [blacksmith, of Hartland,] assembled, supposed with a design to stop the Court. The Sheriff [Benjamin Wait,] and State's Attorney, [Stephen Jacobs,] waited on them, ordered them to disperse, and read the riot act, &c. The insurgents finding their views bafled, dispersed, and the court proceeded to business without molestation.

The same paper of the 20th instant [Nov. 1786] mentions, that at their late session [Nov. 14 1786] of the Superior Court Robert Morrison was taken for a riot.[1] He plead guilty and threw himself on the mercy of the court, who sentenced him to suffer one month's imprisonment, procure bonds of one hundred pounds for his good behaviour for two years, pay a fine of ten pounds and costs of suit. The mob hearing of the matter, sent to their friends & assembled at the house of Captain Lull, in Hartland, to the number of 30 or 40 under arms, intending a rescue. The court being informed of this, ordered the Sheriff to collect assistance, proceed to the place

* E. P. Walton, ed., *Records of the Governor and Council of the State of Vermont*, 8 vols. (Montpelier, 1873–80), III, 366–375.
[1] Present Paul Spooner, chief judge, Nathaniel Niles, Nathaniel Chipman, and Luke Knoulton.

and conduct the insurgents to prison, which, after a short scuffle with bayonets, the breeches of guns, clubs, &c., was happily effected without the loss of a life.[2] Twenty-seven of the insurgents were taken and bro't to goal, most of whom plead guilty and were sentenced to pay fines, costs of court, and procure bonds for their good behaviour for one year.

On hearing of other hostile movements, the millitia were called for and turned out in such numbers, that the insurgents did not think proper to make their appearance.[3]

Bennington, Nov. 27 [1786.]

Copy of a letter to the Printers, dated RUTLAND, Nov. 23.

On Tuesday the 21st instant, the honorable county court for the county of Rutland, met according to law. At the same time there appeared a considerable number of people about the court-house, some of whom were armed with bludgeons &c. The court was opened at 11 o'clock A. M. and adjourned to 2 o'clock P. M. Soon after the adjournment, several persons, who called themselves a committee from the people, waited on the judges of the court, with a petition requesting them to adjourn without day. The committee were informed that after calling the docket, and attending to the necessary business of the day, their request should be taken under consideration. No sooner was the court opened in the afternoon, than a certain Col. Lee [Col. Thomas, of Rutland], who not long since, had discharged himself from prison, by being admitted to the poor man's oath, followed by about an hundred malcontents, rushed into the court-house, and, in a most insolent and riotous manner, began to harrangue and threaten the court, for not adjourning agreeably to the request of their committee. The court ordered the sheriff to adjourn 'till the next day at 9 o'clock in the morning, which was done: The mob then refused to let the court depart from the court-house; called for arms, which were immediately brought them from a neighbouring house, where it seems they were lodged for the occasion: centries were placed at the doors and around the house, and the sheriff, judges and a number of gentlemen attending the court, were made prisoners, and kept in close confinement for about two hours. The mob, finding the judges not easy to be intimidated, then suffered them to depart. The committee again waited on the judges at their lodgings, and renewed their request and received for answer that it could not be complied with; that not only their oath and duty, but the honor and dignity of government, obliged them to proceed to the necessary business of the court. This answer, through the insinuations of designing men, so irritated the rioters, that they resolved, at all

[2] Sheriff Waite and State's attorney Jacobs were both wounded, but not severely.

[3] *Vermont Gazette,* Nov. 27, 1786.

hazards, to prevent the sitting of the court the next day. With an armed force they took possession of the court-house, sent dispatches for a reinforcement of their party, &c. In the meantime orders were sent to Col. [Isaac] Clark and [Stephen] Pearl, and Lieutenant Colonel [John] Spafford, by the sheriff, to raise the militia of the county without loss of time, to come to his assistance in support of government, with three days provision.

These orders were given about 8 or 9 o'clock in the evening, and were executed with such dispatch, that by nine o'clock the next morning, Col. Clark and Pearl appeared with sufficient force to protect the court from any further insult. The militia continually coming from every quarter, the mob thought best to leave the court-house early in the morning, but continued on the ground, to the number of about 150, all day; but made no attempt to stop the court. Just at evening, seven or eight of their leaders were taken and committed to goal; Lee, however, had made his escape. Captain [Benjamin] Cooley of Pittsford, who commanded about 30 or 40 of the insurgents, had retired to a house [Roswell Post's,] about a mile distant from the court-house. Capt. [Noah] Lee of the horse and Lieutenant James Sawyer, a volunteer, were sent with a party of sixteen men, to take and secure them. The insurgents finding themselves in danger, made considerable resistance; several guns were discharged on both sides. But the affair was conducted with so much prudence and firmness on the part of government, that the whole of Capt. Cooley's party, except 2 or 3, who made their escape at a window, were made prisoners. One man only, on the part of government, received a slight wound; one of the mob had had his arm broke in attempting to escape. Several stragglers have since been taken up. The court are now on their trial. Most of the mob were boys, and men of low character, who most probably have been misguided by the base insinuations of a few pestilent demagogues.

Both officers and soldiers on this occasion behaved with the greatest prudence, firmness and determination, which reflects the highest honor on themselves, and merits the warmest thanks of all honest men.

The foregoing account covers substantially the events of the 21st and 22d of November. From a detailed account of succeeding events in Caverly's *History of Pittsford* the following is gathered. On the 23d, Jonathan Fassett, Ebenezer Drury, Dan Barnard, Reuben Allen, Jonathan Swift, Simeon Tupper, Jonathan Rowley, Benjamin Cooley, all of Pittsford, Gideon Horton, Nathan Daniels, of Brandon, and William Roberts, Benjamin Whipple and Silas Mead, of Rutland, were arraigned before the court on an information filed by the state's attorney, and all but

Rowley and Horton were tried, convicted, and sentenced to fines of from £25 to £6 each, to pay costs £1 2 6 each, and to give bonds for good behavior in sums from £150 to £50 each. The highest fine and bond were exacted of Jonathan Fassett, thus marking him as a leading man in the affair. The delinquents declared themselves dissatisfied with the judgment and were permitted to enter an appeal to the then next session of the Superior Court.

The rebellion being considered effectually crushed, on Saturday afternoon [25th] the militia were assembled, and after being addressed by Col. Clark were discharged. But it was so near dark that they remained over night, and on Sabbath morning started for home. As the militia, returning westward, arrived at Pine Hill, they were informed that some two hundred malcontents were assembled at Col. James Mead's, west of Otter Creek. On the reception of this intelligence the Court issued orders for the immediate recall of the militia and for reinforcements from other parts of the county. Col. Pearl, who had gone southward, immediately returned with the militia under his command, and receiving large reinforcements from the west, halted at Blanchard's Corners in West Rutland, while the militia from the east proceeded to Center Rutland and, placing a strong guard at Otter Creek bridge, halted there during the day, thus placing the insurgents in a very unenviable position between two formidable forces. During the latter part of the preceding week, some of the most active in instigating the rebellion, had traversed the neighboring towns, falsely charging the Court with dealing fraudulently with the Regulators, and with treating the prisoners with the most outrageous cruelty. The result of these charges was that even the most candid and conservative portion of the people were aroused to the highest state of indignation. Acting from the impulse of feeling created by what they were made to believe were the acts of an unjust and tyrannical Court, the assemblage at Col. Mead's had convened to inaugurate active measures for redressing their wrongs. Sunday was improved by several friends of law and order, in efforts to convince the malcontents that many of the evils of which they complained did not exist; that for such as did exist, the Court was in no way responsible; that the prisoners had been kindly treated; and that the Court and the government had a common interest in doing all in their power to relieve the sufferings of the people. They were told that they had been misinformed, that they had been imposed upon by a few artful and designing men, and that the course they were pursuing, if persisted in, must inevitably result in bloodshed and ruin. These efforts were attended with gratifying success; the Regulators were convinced that they had been made the dupes of a gross imposition; and as candid and honest men they not only abandoned the object of their enterprise, but even joined the militia under Col. Clark in defence of the Court and the laws. Monday morning, all being again quiet, and no further use for the militia being anticipated, they received the thanks of the Court and were dismissed.

An Act for the prevention and punishment of Riots disorders and contempt of authority.—Passed March 8th 1787.

For the better Suppressing of Riots disorders and contempt of authority.

Be it enacted, &c. that if any person or persons shall impede or hinder any officer judicial or executive civil or military under the authority of this State in the Execution of his office he or they shall on conviction thereof pay a fine not exceeding fifty pounds each and if any person who shall be thereof convicted shall not be of sufficient ability to pay such fine and costs of prosecution it shall be in the power of the Court before whom such conviction shall be had to assign such person in service to any Citizen of this State for so long time as shall be sufficient for payment of the fine and costs aforesaid. And if any person shall be a second time convicted of the like offence he shall pay a fine not exceeding fifty pounds and shall be imprisoned in any Goal in this State for one whole year and if he be not of sufficient ability to pay such fine and cost he shall be liable at the expiration of his said imprisonment to be assigned in service as aforesaid.

And be it further enacted, &c. that if any person or persons shall directly or indirectly break open or aid or assist in breaking open any Goal or place of confinement wherein any prisoners shall be confined by the authority of this State he or they shall on conviction thereof pay a fine of fifty pounds to the Treasurer of the County where such offence shall be committed and lie in prison six months and for a second offence of a like nature shall pay a fine of fifty pounds & be imprisoned one year.

And be it further enacted, &c. that when three persons or more shall come or assemble themselves together to the intent to do any unlawful act with force and violence against the person of another or against his possession or goods wrongfully or to do any unlawful act against the peace or to the manifest terror of the people and being required or commanded by any of the civil authority by proclamation to be made in the form herein after directed shall not disperse themselves and peaceably depart to their habitations or lawful business or being so assembled as aforesaid shall do any unlawful act against the person possession or goods of any man or against the Peace and be thereof convicted before any Court proper to try the same shall be punished by fine not exceeding thirty pounds or imprisonment not exceeding six months and pay cost of prosecution.

That the order and form of proclamation mentioned shall be as follows, That is to say the person authorized by this act shall among or as near as he or they can safely come to said rioters with a loud voice command or order silence to be made whilst proclamation is making and after that shall openly and with a loud voice make proclamation in these words or like in effect viz. "In the name of the State of Vermont I command all persons being assembled immediately to disperse themselves and depart to their habitations or other lawful business upon the pains contained in the law of this State entitled 'an act for the prevention and punishment of Riots Disorders and contempt of authority.' "

And every Justice of Peace, Sheriff, Deputy Sheriff or Constable within their respective jurisdictions are hereby authorized, impowered, and required on notice or knowledge of any such unlawful and riotous assembly to resort to the place where such assembly shall be and there make proclamation as aforesaid.

Be it further enacted, &c. that if such persons so unlawfully assembled, or any three or more of them after proclamation made as aforesaid shall continue together and not disperse themselves that it shall and may be lawful to and for every Justice of the Peace, Sheriff, Deputy Sheriff or Constable where such riotous assembly shall be and to and for every other person or persons who shall be commanded to be assisting to such Justice of the Peace, Sheriff, Deputy Sheriff or Constable (who are hereby authorized and impowered to command all or any of the Inhabitants of this State to be assisting them therein) to seize and apprehend and they are hereby required to seize and apprehend such persons so unlawfully and riotously continuing together after proclamation made as aforesaid and forthwith to carry the persons so apprehended before some Justice of the Peace in order to their being proceeded against according to Law.

And if any of the persons so unlawfully and riotously assembled and continuing together as aforesaid to the number of twelve for the space of one hour after proclamation made as aforesaid shall happen to be killed maimed or hurt in dispersing or apprehending or in endeavouring to disperse or apprehend them by reason of their resisting the persons so dispersing or endeavouring to disperse or apprehend them then every such Justice of the Peace Sheriff Deputy Sheriff or Constable and all and singular the persons aiding or assisting to them or any of them shall be freed discharged and indemnified from any bill complaint indictment or action that may be commenced against him or them on that account.

Be it further enacted, &c. that if any person or persons do or shall forcibly wilfully and knowingly oppose obstruct or in any manner wilfully and knowingly oppose let hinder or hurt any person or persons that shall begin or attempt to make proclamation hereby directed to be made whereby such proclamation shall not be made and be thereof convicted by due course of Law he or they shall forfeit or suffer in manner and form as last aforesaid.

And that all and every such person or persons so being unlawfully and riotously assembled to the number of three or more to whom proclamation should or ought to be made if the same had not been hindered as aforesaid shall likewise in case they or any of them to the number of three or more shall continue together and not immediately disperse themselves after such let or hindrance so made having knowledge thereof and be thereof convicted in due course of Law shall forfeit and pay a fine not exceeding thirty pounds or be imprisoned six months and pay cost as aforesaid.

Provided always that no person or persons shall be punished by virtue of this act unless prosecution be commenced within six months after the offence is committed.

At the same session three acts were passed specially pertinent to the exigencies of the time: one making neat cattle, beef, pork, sheep, wheat, rye, and corn a lawful tender; another providing for the fulfillment of contracts past due according to the original intent of the parties; and the third putting subjects of the United States upon the same footing, in suits at law, in which the citizens of Vermont were put by the laws of the respective states. Moreover, in the general revision of the statutes at that session, due regard to the grievances of the people was indicated in various statutes, one of them being a reorganization of the whole judicial system. By thus tempering justice with mercy, public order was tained, and the government was enabled to render assistance to Massachusetts in bringing her rebellious citizens into subjection to the civil power.

36. Reports on Internal Conditions, I: John Jay to George Washington, June 27, 1786 *

Philadelphia, June 27, 1786.

Dear Sir,

. . . It is too true that the treaty has been violated. On such occasions I think it better fairly to confess and correct errors than attempt to deceive ourselves and others by fallacious, though plausible, palliations and excuses. To oppose popular prejudices, to censure the proceedings, and expose the improprieties of States, is an unpleasant task, but it must be done. Our affairs seem to lead to some crisis, some revolution—something that I cannot foresee or conjecture. I am uneasy and apprehensive; more so than during the war. Then we had a fixed object, and though the means and time of obtaining it were often problematical, yet I did firmly believe we should ultimately succeed, because I was convinced that justice was with us. The case is now altered; we are going and doing wrong, and therefore I look forward to evils and calamities, but without being able to guess at the instrument, nature, or measure of them.

That we shall again recover, and things again go well, I have no doubt. Such a variety of circumstances would not, almost miraculously, have combined to liberate and make us a nation for transient and unimportant purposes. I therefore believe that we are yet to become a great and respectable people; but when or how, the spirit of prophesy can only discern.

There doubtless is much reason to think and to say that we

* H. P. Johnston (ed.), *Correspondence and Public Papers of John Jay*, III, 203–205.

are wofully and, in many instances, wickedly misled. Private rage for property suppresses public considerations, and personal rather than national interests have become the great objects of attention. Representative bodies will ever be faithful copies of their originals, and generally exhibit a checkered assemblage of virtue and vice, of abilities and weakness.

The mass of men are neither wise nor good, and the virtue like the other resources of a country, can only be drawn to a point and exerted by strong circumstances ably managed, or a strong government ably administered. New governments have not the aid of habit and hereditary respect, and being generally the result of preceding tumult and confusion do not immediately acquire stability or strength. Besides, in times of commotion, some men will gain confidence and importance, who merit neither, and who, like political mountebanks, are less solicitous about the health of their nostrums and prescriptions.

New York was rendered less federal by the opinions of the late President of Congress. This is a singular, though not unaccountable fact—indeed, human actions are seldom inexplicable.

What I most fear is, that the better kind of people, by which I mean the people who are orderly and industrious, who are content with their situations and not uneasy in their circumstances, will be led by the insecurity of property, the loss of confidence in their rulers, and the want of public faith and rectitude, to consider the charms of liberty as imaginary and delusive. A state of fluctuation and uncertainty must disgust and alarm such men, and prepare their minds for almost any change that may promise them quiet and security.

Be pleased to make my compliments to Mrs. Washington, and be assured that I am, with the greatest respect and esteem, dear sir,

Your obedient and humble servant,
JOHN JAY

37.   Reports on Internal Conditions, II: George Washington to Henry Lee, October 31, 1786*

Mt. Vernon, 31 October 1786

My Dear Sir,

. . . The picture which you have exhibited, and the accounts which are published of the commotions and temper of numerous bodies in the eastern States, are equally to be lamented and deprecated. They exhibit a melancholy proof of what our transatlantic foe has predicted; and of another thing perhaps, which is still more to be regretted, and is yet more unaccountable, that mankind, when left to themselves, are unfit for their own government. I am mortified beyond expression when I view the clouds that have spread over the brightest morn that ever dawned upon any country. In a word, I am lost in amazement when I behold what intrigue, the interested views of desperate characters, ignorance, and jealousy of the minor part, are capable of effecting, as a scourge on the major part of our fellow citizens of the Union; for it is hardly to be supposed that the great body of the people, though they will not act, can be so shortsighted or enveloped in darkness, as not to see rays of a distant sun through all this mist of intoxication and folly.

You talk, my good sir, of employing influence to appease the present tumults in Massachusetts. I know not where that influence is to be found, or, if attainable, that it would be a proper remedy for the disorders. *Influence* is no *government*. Let us have one by which our lives, liberties, and properties will be

* J. C. Fitzpatrick (ed.), *Writings of George Washington*, 39 vols. (Washington, 1931–44), XXIX, 33–35.

secured, or let us know the worst at once. Under these impressions, my humble opinion is, that there is a call for decision. Know precisely what the insurgents aim at. If they have *real* grievances, redress them if possible; or acknowledge the justice of them, and your inability to do it in the present moment. If they have not, employ the force of government against them at once. If this is inadequate, *all* will be convinced that the superstructure is bad, or wants support. To be more exposed in the eyes of the world, and more contemptible than we already are, is hardly possible. To delay one or the other of these, is to exasperate on the one hand, or to give confidence on the other, and will add their numbers; for, like snow-balls, such bodies increase by every movement, unless there is something in the way to obstruct and crumble them before the weight is too great and irresistible.

These are my sentiments. Precedents are dangerous things. Let the reins of government then be braced and held with a steady hand, and every violation of the Constitution be reprehended. If defective, let it be amended, but not suffered to be trampled upon whilst it has an existence.

38. Reports on Internal Conditions, III: *Mémoire* of the French Chargé d'Affaires at Philadelphia Louis-Guillaume Otto to the Comte de Vergennes, May 17, 1785 *

. . . *Would the dissolution of the Confederation be prejudicial to France?*

The Congress is so to speak the depository of all the obligations that the United States have towards France; it is above all

* *Mémoire* in Correspondance Politique, États-Unis, XXIX, Archives des Affaires Étrangères, Paris.

Congress which has contracted the public debts, and is obligated to pay them. In spite of the continual rotation of its members, the sentiment there is rarely unfavorable to us. Gratitude, respect, unlimited confidence in His Majesty's intentions have always characterized the resolutions of that assembly. It is accustomed to regard the alliance as the guardian of America's liberty, to be attached to our interests, to seek our counsels, to conform to our views, for a happy experience has taught them that we seek only the security and happiness of our allies.

The dissolution of the American Confederation would deprive us of this advantage: the states would probably divide into two parts, the Hudson River forming the separation. The New Englanders next to Canada, stirred up by English emissaries, impatient to distinguish themselves by long-distance expeditions, finding themselves too confined in their land and too poor not to be mortified by the insulting luxury of the people to the south of them, whom they derisively call the nabobs of America, having all the effervescence of a newly-born republic and all the uneasiness of a people used to carrying arms, would become the Spartans of the New World, at least they would have their ambition, without having all their virtues. On the other hand, the southern states, enervated by equally pernicious extremes of wealth and misery, weakened by a burning sun and by the very vastness of their land, unable to oppose a torrent of armed republicans except with troops of timid slaves, would be obliged to beg our help to save them from the rapacity of their neighbors. Whether we chose sides in these wars which would have to take place, or whether we remained neutral, we would have one or the other faction against us.

England would act the minute we declared ourselves, and our commerce would find itself excluded from half of the posts of the continent; instead of useful we would have only onerous allies, whose moves in our favor would be strongly offset by those of the English. The public debt would be lost to us, all the bonds which attach us to the Americans would be imperceptibly broken, and instead of their viewing us with a lively sense of gratitude, motivated by the national interest and the preservation of the states, they would see no more in the alliance than a weak political convenience subject to the variations which always accompany such precarious liaisons.

But let the integrity of the Confederation be protected, let the entire mass of the states rest on a single center and keep its force, let the interests of all the members of the Union discussed in a general assembly merge and be directed toward the same goal as the result of an amicable and constant communication, let the characteristics of the different peoples be modified and softened, let all the members of the Confederation remain convinced that they can count upon His Majesty's protection only when they are closely united: the overall picture will change. Then the national interest will be preserved and grow stronger, its relationships with us grow more firm; in time the power of habit will strengthen the *raison d'état;* the reimbursement of sums owed us will be assured; our commerce will share advantageously with all the nations of the world the crops of America; our islands, our fisheries will be protected from all piracy by the same people who, because of their proximity, are most to be feared; in the case of war with England we can hope for the help of a crowd of privateers which love of gain and the natural inclination of the nation will bring out of all the ports of the continent; our fleets will find sure and convenient winter harbors and our crews refreshments of all sorts, our shipbuilders masts, ropes, and naval ammunition in abundance.

Such are the advantages we may expect from the American Revolution and from the harmony that will reign among the different members of the Confederation. We are therefore essentially interested in the preservation of Congress; and, however limited the influence of Chevalier Otto may be, he will probably be ordered to do all in his power to maintain the union in full force and on all occasions express the King's desire that the integrity of the Confederation be preserved. But, in order to give added weight to the Chevalier's arguments, perhaps it will be thought advisable to authorize him to hint that the alliance will depend on that union, that His Majesty did not treat separately with the northern states or those of the south, that only the thirteen states collectively have the right to claim His Majesty's allegiance, and that after the dissolution of the federal system nothing could stop English invasions in the north or Spanish ones in the south.

This matter is perhaps the most important of all those which can interest us in America, and there is none in which our cause and that of the United States are more closely linked and more clearly tend to the same goal, although for different motives. The vast area which the American states encompass certainly will not always remain united; the Greek republics were too small not to be shaken up by small shocks; these will prove too large to be governed by one single leader. When a growing population will have brought life to all parts of America and when innumerable plows will have made the wilderness productive, the widely dispersed inhabitants of which at the present moment already aspire to independence—when the rivers made navigable will have promoted industry and commerce, when resultant wealth will spawn avarice, ambition, and intrigue, three or four powerful kingdoms will perhaps emerge from the debris of this popular government.

The dissolution of the Confederation must therefore occur in time, but it appears to be to our interest to prevent it as long as possible. Foreign powers will perhaps attempt to stir up a general ferment in America and to poison the very source of the country's happiness; corruption will subtly infect the people's institutions, and weaken patriotism; and the government will be torn by cabals and factions; then it will be indeed glorious for His Majesty to use his influence only to heal the wounds, to soften the misfortunes of the suffering citizens, to bring together the minds, to consolidate a structure erected at the cost of so much bloodshed, and for a second time, become the savior of America.

It is true that several states are now occupied with extending the powers of Congress. Those of the south have ceded considerable territory to it; South Carolina has not only accorded it a five per cent tax but she has also armed that assembly with full powers to regulate her commerce. Pennsylvania, Jersey, and several other states have followed this example, but the obstinacy of Rhode Island, the ill will of the northerners in general, and the lukewarmness of several other members of the Union offer almost insurmountable impediments to Congress's obtaining the full force of which it is capable. Since the beginning of 1783, the yield of customs duties has almost doubled in Massachusetts and in Pennsylvania, and a large part of the state debts could have been wiped out in that interval if the hostility of the representatives of

Rhode Island had not prevented it. It appears to be to our interest, on every possible occasion, to facilitate an arrangement which, in the last analysis, would accelerate the reimbursement of the sums due us and serve as a new link for the Confederation.

39.   Reports on Internal Conditions, IV: French Chargé d'Affaires at Philadelphia Louis-Guillaume Otto to the Comte de Vergennes, June 17, 1786*

My Lord: The low condition into which congress has fallen since the peace begins to excite the attention of true patriots. They see that the federal government cannot remain in its present inaction without endangering the reputation of the United States, and even their independence. The most urgent recommendations of that body are treated by a majority of the states with an indifference which causes lamentations from those who are least susceptible of an interest in public affairs. The department of finance has never been so destitute as at this moment, and one of the commissioners has assured me that he has not the means of meeting current expenses. The most important members of congress are doing all in their power to add to the act of confederation some articles which the present situation of affairs appears to render indispensable. They propose to give to congress executive powers, and the right to make exclusively emissions of paper money and of regulating commerce. They desire, further, the division of that body into two chambers, to prevent an eloquent and ill-intentioned member from carrying away the majority. As to the executive power, the confederation will always be unstable

---

* Correspondance Politique: États-Unis, Ministère des Affaires Étrangères, Paris; translated in George Bancroft, *History of the Formation of the Constitution of the United States of America*, I, 511–512.

until congress shall have carried this important point. The inconsistency of the idea of a sovereign body which has no right but to deliberate and to recommend, in spite of the jealousy of a large number of individuals in America, cannot be concealed. The constant rotation of members of congress is another disadvantage, whose fatal effects are felt more and more; it is difficult for men who merely travel from one end of the continent to the other, and who remain but a few weeks in New York, to master the course of affairs.

Be this as it may, it will require much time and negotiations to correct these defects, and it is impossible to foresee the end of the present embarrassments.

The king of England having renewed, by an order in council of the twenty-fourth of March, the former prohibitions in regard to the importation of American commodities into the British West Indies in American ships, the hopes which were founded on the negotiations of Mr. Adams have vanished. Powerful declamations are the only response to this order, which is here termed a new hostility; and, without remembering the deplorable state of the public treasury and the exhaustion of the finances, there is already talk of arming troops and of seizing by force the posts on the lakes, as if the United States in the present condition of affairs could find the means for such an armament.

40.   Reports on Internal Conditions, V: Phineas Bond to Lord Carmarthen, July 2, 1787*

Philadelphia, July 2nd. 1787

My Lord.

I lately informed your Lordship the Congress had adjourned, and it was probable they would not meet again till the event of the deliberations of the Convention now assembled here, was known. I have since learned some members of Congress are collected at New York and there seems a disposition to form a Congress for the purpose of expediting some matters of urgency. [After May 11, 1787, Congress had no quorum until July 6, when seven States assembled.] . . .

The deliberations of the Convention, my Lord, are conducted with vast secrecy; and nothing is known with accuracy but that their drift is to endeavour to form such a federal constitution, as will give energy and consequence to the union. Whether this is to be done by improving the old governments or by substituting new ones—whether by continuing a power in each State to regulate its internal policy, or to abolish all separate establishments, and to form one grand federal authority, is a matter of consideration which creates much doubt and animadversion.

The task in which this assembly is engaged, my Lord, is attended with no small difficulty: wise and discreet as their determinations *may* be, they have no power to enforce their measures —they *may* recommend such plans as may seem eligible but who

* *Annual Report of the American Historical Association for the Year 1896*, 2 vols. (Washington, 1897), I, 538–540.

are to ratify them? Thirteen different States each claiming and exercising sovereign and independent powers, with various forms of government—great mutual jealousies and interests evidently clashing and interfering with each other. Even in this crisis my Lord when the sober part of the continent looks up to the Convention to prescribe some mode competent to remove existing evils, there is not a complete delegation of the States in Convention—two of the thirteen are not represented, New Hampshire did appoint delegates, but as no fund was provided for their expenses and support they declined attending—The Assembly of Rhode I. positively refused to appoint, and when the motion was again lately agitated, it was negatived by a majority of 17 members [June 11, 1787].

It is plain my Lord, things cannot long remain as they are; there is an universal relaxation of laws and justice, and a total want of energy throughout the States.

In Mass^{ts}. Bay the governor's message to the assembly, of the 5th of June represents the alarming situation and complexion of public affairs there, from the frequent incursions made into that State by the insurgents with an intention to plunder and carry off the friends of Government.—In some instances they had succeeded and it had become necessary to station detachments of the soldiery, in particular towns to guard the friends of the Government.

In the State of Pennsylvania, where the administration of justice is upon a footing superior to most of the States and the police of the country tolerably regulated, a law lately passed directing the mode of selling and granting lands in the county of Luzerne: this law was deemed oppressive, by persons who had claims on the lands, and, at a town meeting at Easton, in the county of Northampton, it was resolved the payment of taxes should be withheld till the obnoxious law should be repealed.

41.   Reports on Internal Conditions, VI: The Connecticut Wits, *The Anarchiad*, 1786–1787 *

Faction

Behold those veterans worn with want and care,
    Their sinews stiffened silvered o'er their hair,
Weak in their steps of age, they move forlorn,
Their toils forgotten by the sons of scorn;
This hateful truth still aggravates the pain,
In vain they conquered, and they bled in vain.

Go then, ye remnants of inglorious wars,
Disown your marks of merit, hide your scars,
Of lust, of power, of titled pride accused,
Steal to your graves dishonored and abused.
    For see, proud Faction waves her flaming brand,
And discord riots o'er the ungrateful land;
Lo, to the North a wild adventurous crew
In desperate mobs the savage state renew;
Each felon chief his maddening thousands draws,
And claims bold license from the bond of laws;
In other states the chosen sires of shame,
Stamp their vile knaveries with a legal name;
In honor's seat the sons of meanness swarm,
And senates base, the work of mobs perform,
To wealth, to power the sons of union rise,

* "American Antiquities No. X," *New Haven Gazette and Connecticut Magazine*, May 24, 1787.

While foes deride you and while friends despise.
     Stand forth, ye traitors, at your country's bar,
Inglorious authors of intestine war,
What countless mischiefs from their labors rise!
Pens dipped in gall, and lips inspired with lies!
Ye sires of ruin, prime detested cause
Of bankrupt faith, annihilated laws,
Of selfish systems, jealous, local schemes,
And unioned empire lost in empty dreams;
Your names, expanding with your growing crime,
Shall float disgustful down the stream of time,
Each future age applaud the avenging song,
And outraged nature vindicate the wrong.
     Yes, there are men, who, touched with heavenly fire,
Beyond the confines of these climes aspire,
Beyond the praises of a tyrant age,
To live immortal in the patriot page;
Who greatly dare, though warning worlds oppose,
To pour just vengeance on their country's foes. . . .
     Yet what the hope? the dreams of congress fade,
The federal union sinks in endless shade,
Each feeble call, that warns the realms around,
Seems the faint echo of a dying sound,
Each requisition wafts in fleeting air,
And not one state regards the powerless prayer.
     Ye wanton states, by heaven's best blessings cursed,
Long on the lap of fostering luxury nursed,
What fickle frenzy raves, what visions strange,
Inspire your bosoms with the lust of change?
And frames the wish to fly from fancied ill,
And yield your freedom to a monarch's will?
     Go view the lands to lawless power a prey,
Where tyrants govern with unbounded sway;
See the long pomp in gorgeous state displayed,
The tinselled guards, the Squadroned horse parade;
See heralds gay with emblems on their vest,
In tissued robes tall beauteous pages drest;
Where moves the pageant, throng unnumbered slaves,
Lords, dukes, and princes, titulary knaves

Confusedly shine, the purple gemmed with stars,
Sceptres, and globes, and crowns, and rubied cars,
On gilded orbs the thundering chariots rolled,
Steeds snorting fire, and champing bits of gold,
Prance to the trumpet's voice—while each assumes
A loftier gait, and lifts his neck of plumes.
High on the moving throne, and near the van,
The tyrant rides, the chosen scourage of man;
Clairons, and flutes, and drums his way prepare,
And shouting millions rend the conscious air;
Millions, whose ceaseless toils the pomp sustain,
Whose hour of stupid joy repays an age of pain.

From years of darkness springs the regal line,
Hereditary kings by right divine:
'Tis theirs to riot on all nature's spoils,
For them with pangs unblest the peasant toils,
For them the earth prolific teems with grain,
Theirs, the dread labors of the devious main,
Annual for them the wasted land renews
The gifts oppressive, and extorted dues.
For them when slaughter spreads the gory plains,
The life-blood gushes from a thousand veins,
While the dull herd, of earth-born pomp afraid,
Adore the power that coward meanness made. . . .

Nor less abhorred the certain woe that waits
The giddy rage of democratic states;
Whose popular breath, high blown in restless tide,
No laws can temper, and no reason guide;
An equal sway their mind indignant spurns,
To wanton change the bliss of freedom turns,
Led by wild demagogues the factious crowd,
Mean, fierce, imperious, insolent and loud,
Nor fame nor wealth nor power nor system draws,
They see no object and perceive no cause,
But feel by turns, in one disastrous hour,
The extremes of license and the extremes of power.

What madness prompts, or what ill-omened fates,
Your realm to parcel into petty states?
Shall lordly Hudson part contending powers?

And broad Potomac lave two hostile shores?
Must Allegany's sacred summits bear
The impious bulwarks of perpetual war?
His hundred streams receive your heroes slain?
And bear your sons inglorious to the main?
Will states cement by feebler bonds allied?
Or join more closely as they more divide?
Will this vain scheme bid restless factions cease?
Check foreign wars or fix internal peace?
Call public credit from her grave to rise?
Or gain in grandeur what they lose in size?
In this weak realm can countless kingdoms start,
Strong with new force in each divided part?
While empire's head, divided into four,
Gains life by severance of diminished power?
So when the philosophic hand divides
The full grown polypus in genial tides,
Each severed part, informed with latent life,
Acquires new vigor from the friendly knife,
O'er peopled sands the puny insects creep,
Till the next wave absorbs them in the deep.

What then remains? must pilgrim freedom fly
From these loved regions to her native sky?
When the fair fugitive the orient chased,
She fixed her seat beyond the watery wast;
Her docile sons (enough of power resigned,
And natural rites in social leagues combined)
In virtue firm, though jealous in her cause,
Gave senates force and energy to laws,
From ancient habit local powers obey,
You feel no reverence for one general sway,
For breach of faith no keen compulsion feel,
And feel no interest in the federal weal.
But know, ye favored race, one potent head,
Must rule your states, and strike your foes with dread,
The finance regulate, the trade control,
Live through the empire, and accord the whole.

Ere death invades, and night's deep curtain falls,
Through ruined realms the voice of Union calls,

Loud as the trump of heaven through darkness roars,
When gyral gusts entomb Caribbean towers,
When nature trembles through the deeps convulsed,
And ocean foams from craggy cliffs repulsed,
On you she calls! attend the warning cry,
"Ye live united, or divided die." . . .
    But chief the race allured by fleeting fame,
Who seek on earth the politicians name;
Auspicious race! whom folly joins to bless,
And wealth and honor crown with glad success;
Formed, like balloons, by emptiness to rise
On pop'lar gales, to waft them through the skies . . .
See, from the shades, on tiny pinions swell
And rise, the young DEMOCRACY of *hell!*
Before their face the *powers of Congress* fade
And *public credit* sinks, an empty shade;
Wild severance rages, wars intestine spread.
Their boasted UNION hides her dying head;
The forms of government in ruin hurl'd,
Reluctant empire quits the western world.

Chapter XII

ANNAPOLIS AND PHILADELPHIA

By 1786, many leaders, dissatisfied with the weakness of the Confederation, were considering ways of amending the Articles so as to strengthen the central government. Acting upon the resolutions of the Mount Vernon Conference of 1785 in which commissioners from Maryland and Virginia discussed the navigation of the Potomac, James Madison pushed through a measure in the Virginia legislature calling for the appointment of commissioners to meet with representatives of all the states to consider the commercial problems of the nation in general. Although little was accomplished, since only five states sent delegates to Annapolis, the persons attending adopted a report calling for a gathering of commissioners from all the states the following May at Philadelphia. This was the first step toward the summoning of a constitutional convention.

Although the delegates to the Philadelphia Convention had ostensibly assembled to revise the Articles of Confederation, the presentation of the Virginia or Randolph Plan early in the proceedings foreshadowed the possibility of far greater change in the national structure. The fifteen resolves put forth by Randolph outlined the basis for a new national government. The Plan called for a national executive, judiciary, and two-house legislature, one branch to be elected by the people, the other (the Senate) to be chosen by the first branch. More than any other proposal brought before the Convention, the Virginia Plan formed the basis of the new constitution.

Two weeks after the Virginia Plan was introduced, William Paterson placed before the Convention the New Jersey Plan, which would have sustained the sovereignty of the respective states. Fearing a strong central government, Paterson proposed the creation of a unicameral legislature where the states were to have an equal vote with no regard to population and an executive council to be chosen by Congress. "If the Confederacy was radically wrong," he said, "let us return to our states and obtain *larger powers, not assume them ourselves. . . . We have no power to vary the idea of equal sovereignty." The New Jersey Plan had the support of many states' rights advocates at the Convention, but most of its provisions were eventually rejected.*

After three days of debate the Convention voted to establish a national government as visualized in the Virginia Plan, and a crucial compromise was agreed to on the subject of representation in the national legislature. Sponsored by Roger Sherman of Connecticut, the proposal provided that representation in the lower house be proportional to population, while in the upper house the states enjoy an equality of representation. Having accepted this proposal, the Convention moved forward, settling such other outstanding issues as the length of terms of Senators, Representatives, and the President, and conferring upon Congress the power to regulate foreign and interstate commerce. In agreement on all essentials, the Convention named a Committee on Style to prepare a final draft, which was substantially approved on September 17th; thirty-nine out of forty-two delegates present signed the engrossed copy.

By the terms of Article 7, the Constitution was to become operative when ratified by nine states. The battle now shifted to the state ratifying conventions.

42. Annapolis Convention Report of Proceedings, September 14, 1786*

To the Honorable, the Legislatures of Virginia, Delaware, Pennsylvania, New Jersey, and New York—

The Commissioners from the said States, respectively assembled at Annapolis, humbly beg leave to report.

That, pursuant to their several appointments, they met, at Annapolis in the State of Maryland, on the eleventh day of September Instant, and having proceeded to a Communication of their Powers; they found that the States of New York, Pennsylvania, and Virginia, had, in substance, and nearly in the same terms, authorized their respective Commissioners "to meet such other Commissioners as were, or might be, appointed by the other States in the Union, at such time and place as should be agreed upon by the said Commissioners to take into consideration the trade and commerce of the United States, to consider how far an uniform system in their commercial intercourse and regulations might be necessary to their common interest and permanent harmony, and to report to the several States such an Act, relative to this great object, as when unanimously ratified by them would enable the United States in Congress assembled effectually to provide for the same." . . .

That the State of New Jersey had enlarged the object of their appointment, empowering their Commissioners, "to consider how far an uniform system in their commercial regulations and *other*

* *Documents Illustrative of the Formation of the Union of the American States,* 69th Cong., 1st sess., House Doc. 398 (Washington, 1927), 39 *et seq.*

important matters, might be necessary to the common interest and permanent harmony of the several States," and to report such an Act on the subject, as when ratified by them, "would enable the United States in Congress assembled, effectually to provide for the exigencies of the Union."

That appointments of Commissioners have also been made by the States of New Hampshire, Massachusetts, Rhode Island, and North Carolina, none of whom however have attended; but that no information has been received by your Commissioners, of any appointment having been made by the States of Connecticut, Maryland, South Carolina or Georgia.

That the express terms of the powers of your Commissioners supposing a deputation from all the States, and having for object the Trade and Commerce of the United States, Your Commissioners did not conceive it advisable to proceed on the business of their mission, under the Circumstance of so partial and defective a representation.

Deeply impressed however with the magnitude and importance of the object confided to them on this occasion, your Commissioners cannot forbear to indulge an expression of their earnest and unanimous wish, that speedy measures be taken, to effect a general meeting, of the States, in a future Convention, for the same, and such other purposes, as the situation of public affairs may be found to require.

If in expressing this wish, or in intimating any other sentiment, your Commissioners should seem to exceed the strict bounds of their appointment, they entertain a full confidence, that a conduct, dictated by an anxiety for the welfare of the United States, will not fail to receive an indulgent construction.

In this persuasion, your Commissioners submit an opinion, that the Idea of extending the powers of their Deputies, to other objects, than those of Commerce, which has been adopted by the State of New Jersey, was an improvement on the original plan, and will deserve to be incorporated into that of a future Convention; they are the more naturally led to this conclusion, as in the course of their reflections on the subject, they have been induced to think, that the power of regulating trade is of such comprehensive extent, and will enter so far into the general System of the foederal government, that to give it efficacy, and to obviate questions and doubts concerning its precise nature and limits, may require a correspondent adjustment of other parts of the Foederal System.

That there are important defects in the system of the Foederal Government is acknowledged by the Acts of all those States, which have concurred in the present Meeting; That the defects, upon a closer examination, may be found greater and more numerous, than even these acts imply, is at least so far probable, from the embarrassment which characterise the present State of our national affairs, foreign and domestic, as may reasonably be supposed to merit a deliberate and candid discussion, in some mode, which will unite the Sentiments and Councils of all the States. In the choice of the mode, your Commissioners are of opinion, that a Convention of Deputies from the different States, for the special and sole purpose of entering into this investigation, and digesting a plan for supplying such defects as may be discovered to exist, will be entitled to a preference from considerations, which will occur without being particularised.

Your Commissioners decline an enumeration of those national circumstances on which their opinion respecting the propriety of a future Convention, with more enlarged powers, is founded; as it would be an useless intrusion of facts and observations, most of which have been frequently the subject of public discussion, and none of which can have escaped the penetration of those to whom they would in this instance be addressed. They are however of a nature so serious, as, in the view of your Commissioners, to render the situation of the United States delicate and critical, calling for an exertion of the united virtue and wisdom of all the members of the Confederacy.

Under this impression, Your Commissioners, with the most respectful deference, beg leave to suggest their unanimous conviction that it may essentially tend to advance the interests of the union if the States, by whom they have been respectively delegated, would themselves concur, and use their endeavours to procure the concurrence of the other States, in the appointment of Commissioners, to meet at Philadelphia on the second Monday in May next, to take into consideration the situation of the United States, to devise such further provisions as shall appear to them necessary to render the constitution of the Foederal Government adequate to the exigencies of the Union; and to report such an Act for that purpose to the United States in Congress assembled, as when agreed to, by them, and afterwards confirmed by the Legislatures of every State, will effectually provide for the same.

Though your Commissioners could not with propriety address these observations and sentiments to any but the States they have the honor to represent, they have nevertheless concluded from motives of respect, to transmit copies of this Report to the United States in Congress assembled, and to the executives of the other States.

43. Constitutional Convention of 1787: Virginia or Randolph Plan, May 29, 1787*

1. Resolved that the Articles of Confederation ought to be so corrected and enlarged as to accomplish the objects proposed by their institution; namely "common defence, security of liberty and general welfare."
2. Resolved therefore that the rights of suffrage in the National Legislature ought to be proportioned to the Quotas of contribution, or to the number of free inhabitants, as the one or the other rule may seem best in different cases.
3. Resolved that the National Legislature ought to consist of two branches.

* G. Hunt and J. B. Scott (eds.), *Debates in the Federal Convention of 1787 Reported by James Madison* (New York, 1920), 23 *et seq.* For variant texts see *Documents Illustrative of the Formation of the Union of the American States,* 953 *et seq.*

4. Resolved that the members of the first branch of the National Legislature ought to be elected by the people of the several States every   for the terms of; to be of the age of   years at least, to receive liberal stipends by which they may be compensated for the devotion of their time to public service, to be ineligible to any office established by a particular State, or under the authority of the United States, except those peculiarly belonging to the functions of the first branch, during the term of service, and for the space of   after its expiration; to be incapable of reelection for the space of after the expiration of their term of service, and to be subject to recall.

5. Resolved that the members of the second branch of the National Legislature ought to be elected by those of the first, out of a proper number of persons nominated by the individual Legislatures, to be of the age of years at least; to hold their offices for a term sufficient to ensure their independency; to receive liberal stipends, by which they may be compensated for the devotion of their time to public service; and to be ineligible to any office established by a particular State, or under the authority of the United States, except those peculiarly belonging to the functions of the second branch, during the term of service, and for the space of   after the expiration thereof.

6. Resolved that each branch ought to possess the right of originating Acts; that the National Legislature ought to be impowered to enjoy the Legislative Rights vested in Congress by the Confederation and moreover to legislate in all cases to which the separate States are incompetent, or in which the harmony of the United States may be interrupted by the exercise of individual Legislation; to negative all laws passed by the several States, contravening in the opinion of the National Legislature the articles of Union; and to call forth the force of the Union against any member of the Union failing in its duty under the articles thereof.

7. Resolved that a National Executive be instituted; to be chosen by the National Legislature for the terms of   years; to receive punctually, at stated times, a fixed compensation for the services rendered, in which no increase or diminution shall be made so as to affect the Magistracy, existing at the time of the increase or diminution, and to be ineligible a second time; and

that besides a general authority to execute the National laws, it ought to enjoy the Executive rights vested in Congress by the Confederation.

8. Resolved that the Executive and a convenient number of the National Judiciary, ought to compose a Council of revision with authority to examine every act of the National Legislature before it shall operate, and every act of a particular Legislature before a Negative thereon shall be final; and that the dissent of the said Council shall amount to a rejection, unless the Act of the National Legislature be passed again, or that of a particular Legislature be again negatived by   of the members of each branch.

9. Resolved that a National Judiciary be established to consist of one or more supreme tribunals, and of inferior tribunals to be chosen by the National Legislature, to hold their offices during good behaviour; and to receive punctually at stated times fixed compensation for their services, in which no increase or diminution shall be made so as to affect the persons actually in office at the time of such increase or diminution. That the jurisdiction of the inferior tribunals shall be to hear and determine in the first instance, and of the supreme tribunal to hear and determine in the dernier resort, all piracies and felonies on the high seas, captures from an enemy; cases in which foreigners or citizens of other States applying to such jurisdictions may be interested, or which respect the collection of the National revenue; impeachments of any National officers, and questions which may involve the national peace and harmony.

10. Resolved that provision ought to be made for the admission of States lawfully arising within the limits of the United States, whether from a voluntary junction of Government and Territory or otherwise, with the consent of a number of voices in the National legislature less than the whole.

11. Resolved that a Republican Government and the territory of each State, except in the instance of a voluntary junction of Government and territory, ought to be guaranteed by the United States to each State.

12. Resolved that provision ought to be made for the continuance of Congress and their authorities and privileges, until a given day after the reform of the articles of Union shall be adopted, and for the completion of all their engagements.

13. Resolved that provision ought to be made for the amendment of the Articles of Union whensoever it shall seem necessary, and that the assent of the National Legislature ought not to be required thereto.

14. Resolved that the Legislative Executive and Judiciary powers within the several States ought to be bound by oath to support the articles of Union.

15. Resolved that the amendments which shall be offered to the Confederation, by the Convention ought at a proper time, or times, after the approbation of Congress to be submitted to an assembly or assemblies of Representatives, recommended by the several Legislatures to be expressly chosen by the people, to consider and decide thereon.

44. Constitutional Convention of 1787: New Jersey or Paterson Plan, June 15, 1787 *

1. Resolved that the Articles of Confederation ought to be so revised, corrected, and enlarged as to render the federal Constitution adequate to the exigencies of Government, and the preservation of the Union.

2. Resolved that in addition to the powers invested in the United States in Congress, by the present existing articles of Confederation, they be authorized to pass acts for raising a revenue, by levying a duty or duties on all goods or merchandizes of foreign growth or manufacture, imported into any part of the United

* G. Hunt and J. B. Scott (eds.), *Debates in the Federal Convention of 1787 Reported by James Madison,* 102–104. For variant texts see *Documents Illustrative of the Formation of the Union of the American States,* 967–968.

States, by Stamps on paper, vellum or parchment, and by a postage on all letters or packages passing through the general post-office, to be applied to such federal purposes as they shall deem proper and expedient; to make rules and regulations for the collection thereof; and the same from time to time, to alter and amend in such manner as they shall think proper: to pass Acts for the regulation of trade and commerce as well with foreign nations as with each other; provided that all punishments, fines, forfeitures and penalties to be incurred for contravening such acts rules and regulations shall be adjudged by the Common law Judiciaries of the State in which any offence contrary to the true intent and meaning of such Acts rules and regulations shall have been committed or perpetrated, with liberty of commencing in the first instance all suits and prosecutions for that purpose, in the superior common law Judiciary in such state, subject nevertheless, for the correction of errors, both in law and fact in rending Judgment, to an appeal to the Judiciary of the United States.

3. Resolved that whenever requisitions shall be necessary, instead of the rule for making requisitions mentioned in the articles of Confederation, the United States in Congress be authorized to make such requisitions in proportion to the whole number of white and other free citizens and inhabitants of every age sex and condition including those bound to servitude for a term of years and three fifths of all other persons not comprehended in the foregoing description, except Indians not paying taxes; that if such requisitions be not complied with, in the time specified therein, to direct the collection thereof in the non-complying States and for that purpose to devise and pass acts directing and authorizing the same; provided that none of the powers hereby vested in the United States in Congress shall be exercised without the consent of at least   States, and in that proportion if the number of Confederated States should hereafter be increased or diminished.

4. Resolved that the United States in Congress be authorized to elect a federal Executive to consist of   persons, to continue in office for the term of years, to receive punctually at stated times a fixed compensation for their services, in which no increase or diminution shall be made so as to affect the persons

composing the Executive at the time of such increase or diminution, to be paid out of the federal treasury; to be incapable of holding any other office or appointment during their time of service and for   years thereafter; to be ineligible a second time, and removeable by Congress on application by a majority of the Executives of the several States; that the Executives besides their general authority to execute the federal acts ought to appoint all federal officers not otherwise provided for, and to direct all military operations; provided that none of the persons composing the federal Executive shall on any occasion take command of any troops so as personally to conduct any enterprise as General or in other capacity.

5. Resolved that a Federal Judiciary be established to consist of a supreme tribunal the Judges of which to be appointed by the Executive, and to hold their offices during good behaviour, to receive punctually at stated times a fixed compensation for their services in which no increase or diminution shall be made so as to affect persons actually in office at the time of such increase or diminution; that the Judiciary so established shall have authority to hear and determine in the first instance on all impeachments of federal officers, and by way of appeal in the dernier resort in all cases touching the rights of Ambassadors, in all cases of captures from an enemy, in all cases of piracies and felonies on the high Seas, in all cases in which foreigners may be interested, in the construction of any treaty or treaties, or which may arise on any of the Acts for regulation of trade, or the collection of the federal Revenue: that none of the Judiciary shall during the time they remain in office be capable of receiving or holding any other office or appointment during the time of service, or for thereafter.

6. Resolved that all Acts of the United States in Congress made by virtue and in pursuance of the powers hereby and by the articles of Confederation vested in them, and all Treaties made and ratified under the authority of the United States, shall be the supreme law of the respective States so far forth as those Acts or Treaties shall relate to the said States or their Citizens, and that the Judiciary of the several States shall be bound thereby in their decisions, any thing in the respective laws of the Individual States to the contrary notwithstanding; and that if any State, or any body of men in any State shall oppose or pre-

vent carrying into execution such acts or treaties, the federal Executive shall be authorized to call forth the power of the Confederated States, or so much thereof as may be necessary to enforce and compel an obedience to such Acts or an observance of such Treaties.

7. Resolved that provision be made for the admission of new States into the Union.

8. Resolved the rule for naturalization ought to be the same in every State.

9. Resolved that a Citizen of one State committing an offence in another State of the Union, shall be deemed guilty of the same offence as if it had been committed by a Citizen of the State in which the offence was committed.

45.   The Constitution of the United States

The Constitutional Convention which convened at Philadelphia on May 25, 1787, completed its monumental work in less than four months. The convention considered (1) the Virginia plan proposed by Edmund Randolph, which went beyond revision of the Articles of Confederation and advocated a new national government with a bicameral legislature representing the states proportionately; (2) an opposing New Jersey plan of William Paterson, which stressed retention of the Confederation but conferred upon Congress the power to tax and regulate foreign and interstate commerce and to name a plural executive without veto. The so-called Connecticut compromise providing for representation to be proportional to population in the lower house, with one vote for each state in the senate, essentially settled the major issue between the large and small states. The convention agreed that each state's representation in the lower house should be based on the total of its white population and three-fifths of its Negro population, and accepted the principle that in the senate each state should have an equal vote. Other provisions were hammered out during the great debate on the draft constitution (August 6 to September 10). The final draft was prepared by Gouverneur Morris. New Hampshire, the ninth state, ratified the Constitution on June 21, 1788. Five states' ratifying conventions had stressed the need for immediate amendments to the Constitution, and in the First Congress James Madison proposed twelve amendments, of which ten were ratified by the states, and composed the Bill of Rights. These became a part of the Constitution on December 15, 1791.

PREAMBLE

We the People of the United States, in Order to form a more perfect Union, establish Justice, insure domestic Tranquility, provide for the common defence, promote the general Welfare, and secure the Blessings of Liberty to ourselves and our Posterity, do ordain and establish this Constitution for the United States of America.

ARTICLE I

Section 1. All legislative Powers herein granted shall be vested in a Congress of the United States, which shall consist of a Senate and House of Representatives.

Section 2. The House of Representatives shall be composed of Members chosen every second Year by the People of the several states, and the Electors in each State shall have the Qualifications requisite for Electors of the most numerous Branch of the State Legislature.

No Person shall be a Representative who shall not have attained to the Age of twenty five Years, and been seven Years a Citizen of the United States, and who shall not, when elected, be an inhabitant of that State in which he shall be chosen.

Representatives and direct Taxes shall be apportioned among the several States which may be included within this Union, according to their respective Numbers, [which shall be determined by adding to the whole Number of free Persons, including those bound to Service for a Term of Years, and excluding Indians not taxed, three fifths of all other Persons.] [1] The actual Enumeration shall be made within three Years after the first Meeting of the Congress of the United States, and within every subsequent Term of ten Years, in such Manner as they shall by law direct. The Number of Representatives shall not exceed one for every thirty Thousand, but each State shall have at Least one Representative; and until such enumeration shall be made, the State of New Hampshire shall be entitled to chuse three, Massachusetts eight, Rhode Island and Providence Plantations one, Connecticut five, New York six, New Jersey four, Pennsylvania eight, Delaware one, Maryland six, Virginia ten, North Carolina five, South Carolina five, and Georgia three.

When vacancies happen in the Representation from any State, the Executive Authority thereof shall issue Writs of Election to fill such Vacancies.

The House of Representatives shall chuse their Speaker and other Officers; and shall have the sole Power of Impeachment.

Section 3. The Senate of the United States shall be composed of two Senators from each State, [chosen by the Legislature thereof,] [2] for six Years; and each Senator shall have one Vote.

Immediately after they shall be assembled in Consequence of the first Election, they shall be divided as equally as may be into three Classes. The Seats of the Senators of the first Class shall be vacated at the Expiration of the second Year, of the second Class at the Expiration of the fourth Year, and of the third Class at the Expiration of the sixth Year, so that one third may be chosen every second Year; [and if Vacancies happen by Resignation, or otherwise, during the Recess of the Legislature of any State, the Executive thereof may make temporary Appointments until the next Meeting of the Legislature, which shall then fill such Vacancies.] [3]

No Person shall be a Senator who shall not have attained to the age of thirty Years, and been nine Years a Citizen of the

[1] Superseded by the Fourteenth Amendment.
[2] Superseded by the Seventeenth Amendment.
[3] Modified by the Seventeenth Amendment.

United States, and who shall not, when elected, be an Inhabitant of that State for which he shall be chosen.

The Vice President of the United States shall be President of the Senate, but shall have no Vote, unless they be equally divided.

The Senate shall chuse their other Officers, and also a President pro tempore, in the Absence of the Vice President, or when he shall exercise the Office of President of the United States.

The Senate shall have the sole Power to try all Impeachments. When sitting for that Purpose, they shall be on Oath or Affirmation. When the President of the United States is tried, the Chief Justice shall preside: and no Person shall be convicted without the Concurrence of two thirds of the Members present.

Judgment in Cases of Impeachment shall not extend further than to removal from office, and disqualification to hold and enjoy any Office of honor, Trust or Profit under the United States: but the Party convicted shall nevertheless be liable and subject to Indictment, Trial, Judgment and Punishment, according to Law.

Section 4. The Times, Places and Manner of holding Elections for Senators and Representatives, shall be prescribed in each State by the Legislature thereof; but the Congress may at any time by Law make or alter such Regulations, except as to the Places of chusing Senators.

[The Congress shall assemble at least once in every Year, and such Meeting shall be on the first Monday in December, unless they shall by Law appoint a different Day.] [4]

Section 5. Each House shall be the Judge of the Elections, Returns and Qualifications of its own Members, and a Majority of each shall constitute a Quorum to do Business; but a smaller Number may adjourn from day to day, and may be authorized to compel the Attendance of absent Members, in such Manner, and under such Penalties as each House may provide.

Each House may determine the Rules of its Proceedings, punish its Members for disorderly Behaviour, and, with the Concurrence of two thirds, expel a Member.

Each House shall keep a Journal of its Proceedings, and from time to time publish the same, excepting such Parts as may in their Judgment require Secrecy; and the Yeas and Nays of the

[4] Superseded by the Twentieth Amendment.

Members of either House on any question shall, at the Desire of one fifth of those Present, be entered on the Journal.

Neither House, during the Session of Congress, shall, without the Consent of the other, adjourn for more than three days, nor to any other Place than that in which the two Houses shall be sitting.

Section 6. The Senators and Representatives shall receive a Compensation for their Services, to be ascertained by Law, and paid out of the Treasury of the United States. They shall in all Cases except Treason, Felony and Breach of the Peace, be privileged from Arrest during their Attendance at the Session of their respective Houses, and in going to and returning from the same; and for any Speech or Debate in either House, they shall not be questioned in any other Place.

No Senator or Representative shall, during the Time for which he was elected, be appointed to any civil Office under the Authority of the United States, which shall have been created, or the Emoluments whereof shall have been encreased during such time; and no Person holding any Office under the United States, shall be a Member of either House during his Continuance in Office.

Section 7. All bills for raising Revenue shall originate in the House of Representatives; but the Senate may propose or concur with Amendments as on other Bills.

Every Bill which shall have passed the House of Representatives and the Senate, shall, before it become a Law, be presented to the President of the United States; If he approve he shall sign it, but if not he shall return it, with his Objections to that House in which it shall have originated, who shall enter the Objections at large on their Journal, and proceed to reconsider it. If after such Reconsideration two thirds of that House shall agree to pass the Bill, it shall be sent, together with the Objections, to the other House, by which it shall likewise be reconsidered, and if approved by two thirds of that House, it shall become a Law. But in all such Cases the Votes of both Houses shall be determined by yeas and Nays, and the Names of the Persons voting for and against the Bill shall be entered on the Journal of each House respectively. If any Bill shall not be returned by the President within ten Days (Sundays excepted) after it shall have been presented to him, the Same shall be a Law, in like Manner as if he had signed it, unless the Congress by their Adjournment prevent its Return, in which Case it shall not be a Law.

Every Order, Resolution, or Vote to which the Concurrence of the Senate and House of Representatives may be necessary (except on a question of Adjournment) shall be presented to the President of the United States; and before the Same shall take Effect, shall be approved by him, or being disapproved by him, shall be repassed by two thirds of the Senate and House of Representatives, according to the Rules and Limitations prescribed in the Case of a Bill.

Section 8. The Congress shall have Power To lay and collect Taxes, Duties, Imposts and Excises, to pay the Debts and provide for the common Defence and general Welfare of the United States; but all Duties, Imposts and Excises shall be uniform throughout the United States;

To borrow Money on the credit of the United States;

To regulate Commerce with foreign Nations, and among the several States, and with the Indian Tribes;

To establish a uniform Rule of Naturalization, and uniform Laws on the subject of Bankruptcies throughout the United States;

To coin Money, regulate the Value thereof, and of foreign Coin, and fix the Standard of Weights and Measures;

To provide for the Punishment of counterfeiting the Securities and current Coin of the United States;

To establish Post Offices and post Roads;

To promote the Progress of Science and useful Arts, by securing for limited Times to Authors and Inventors the exclusive Right to their respective Writings and Discoveries;

To constitute Tribunals inferior to the supreme Court;

To define and punish Piracies and Felonies committed on the high Seas, and Offences against the Law of Nations;

To declare War, grant Letters of Marque and Reprisal, and make Rules concerning Captures on Land and Water;

To raise and support Armies, but no Appropriation of Money to that Use shall be for a longer Term than two Years;

To provide and maintain a Navy;

To make Rules for the Government and Regulation of the land and naval Forces;

To provide for calling forth the Militia to execute the Laws of the Union, suppress Insurrections and repel Invasions;

To provide for organizing, arming, and disciplining, the Militia, and for governing such Part of them as may be employed in the Service of the United States, reserving to the States respectively, the Appointment of the Officers, and the Authority of training the Militia according to the discipline prescribed by Congress;

To exercise exclusive Legislation in all Cases whatsoever, over such District (not exceeding ten Miles square) as may, by Cession of particular States, and the Acceptance of Congress, become the Seat of the Government of the United States, and to exercise like Authority over all Places purchased by the Consent of the Legislature of the State in which the Same shall be, for the Erection of Forts, Magazines, Arsenals, dock-Yards, and other needful Buildings;—And

To make all Laws which shall be necessary and proper for carrying into Execution the foregoing Powers, and all other Powers vested by this Constitution in the Government of the United States, or in any Department or Officer thereof.

Section 9. The Migration or Importation of such Persons as any of the States now existing shall think proper to admit, shall not be prohibited by the Congress prior to the Year one thousand eight hundred and eight, but a Tax or duty may be imposed on such Importation, not exceeding ten dollars for each Person.

The Privilege of the Writ of Habeas Corpus shall not be suspended, unless when in Cases of Rebellion or Invasion the public safety may require it.

No Bill of Attainder or ex post facto Law shall be passed.

No Capitation, or other direct, Tax shall be laid, unless in Proportion to the Census or Enumeration herein before directed to be taken.[5]

No tax or Duty shall be laid on Articles exported from any State.

No Preference shall be given by any Regulation of Commerce

[5] Modified by the Sixteenth Amendment.

or Revenue to the Ports of one State over those of another! nor shall Vessels bound to, or from, one State, be obliged to enter, clear, or pay Duties in another.

No money shall be drawn from the Treasury, but in Consequence of Appropriations made by Law; and a regular Statement and Account of the Receipts and Expenditures of all public Money shall be published from time to time.

No Title of Nobility shall be granted by the United States: And no Person holding any Office of Profit or Trust under them, shall, without the Consent of the Congress, accept any present, Emolument, Office, or Title, of any kind whatever, from any King, Prince, or foreign State.

Section 10. No State shall enter into any Treaty, Alliance, or Confederation; grant Letters of Marque and Reprisal; coin Money; emit Bills of Credit; make any Thing but gold and silver Coin a Tender in Payment of Debts; pass any Bill of Attainder, ex post facto Law, or Law impairing the Obligation of Contracts, or grant any Title of Nobility.

No State shall, without the Consent of the Congress, lay any Imposts or Duties on Imports or Exports, except what may be absolutely necessary for executing its inspection laws; and the net Produce of all Duties and Imposts, laid by any State on Imports or Exports, shall be for the Use of the Treasury of the United States; and all such Laws shall be subject to the Revision, and Control of the Congress.

No State shall, without the Consent of Congress, lay any Duty of Tonnage, keep Troops, or Ships of War in time of Peace, enter into any Agreement or Compact with another State, or with a foreign Power, or engage in War, unless actually invaded, or in such imminent Danger as will not admit of delay.

ARTICLE II

Section 1. The executive Power shall be vested in a President of the United States of America. He shall hold his Office during the Term of four Years, and, together with the Vice President, chosen for the same Term, be elected, as follows.

Each State shall appoint, in such Manner as the Legislature thereof may direct, a Number of Electors, equal to the whole Number of Senators and Representatives to which the State may be entitled in the Congress: but no Senator or Representative, or Person holding an Office of Trust or Profit under the United States, shall be appointed an Elector.

[The Electors shall meet in their respective States, and vote by Ballot for two Persons, of whom one at least shall not be an Inhabitant of the same State with themselves. And they shall make a List of all the Persons voted for, and the Number of Votes for each; which list they shall sign and certify, and transmit sealed to the Seat of the Government of the United States, directed to the President of the Senate. The President of the Senate shall, in the Presence of the Senate and House of Representatives, open all the Certificates, and the Votes shall then be counted. The person having the greatest Number of Votes shall be the President, if such Number be a Majority of the whole Number of Electors appointed; and if there be more than one who have such Majority, and have an equal Number of Votes, then the House of Representatives shall immediately chuse by Ballot one of them for President; and if no Person have a Majority, then from the five highest on the List the said House shall in like Manner chuse the President. But in chusing the President, the Votes shall be taken by States, the Representation from each State having one Vote; A quorum for this purpose shall consist of a Member or Members from two-thirds of the States, and a Majority of all the States shall be necessary to a Choice. In every Case, after the Choice of the President, the Person having the greatest Number of Votes of the Electors shall be the Vice President. But if there should remain two or more who have equal Votes, the Senate chuse from them by Ballot the Vice President.] [6]

The Congress may determine the Time of chusing the Electors, and the Day on which they shall give their Votes; which Day shall be the same throughout the United States.

No Person except a natural born Citizen, or a Citizen of the United States, at the time of the Adoption of this Constitution, shall be eligible to the Office of President; neither shall any Person be eligible to that Office who shall not have attained to the Age of thirty five Years, and been fourteen Years a Resident within the United States.

In case of the Removal of the President from Office, or of his

[6] Superseded by the Twelfth Amendment.

Death, Resignation, or Inability to discharge the Powers and Duties of the said Office, the Same shall devolve on the Vice President, and the Congress may by Law provide for the Case of Removal, Death, Resignation or Inability, both of the President and Vice President, declaring what Officer shall then act as President, and such Officer shall act accordingly, until the Disability be removed, or a President shall be elected.[7]

The President shall, at stated Times receive for his Services, a Compensation, which shall neither be encreased nor diminished during the Period for which he shall have been elected, and he shall not receive within that Period any other Emolument from the United States, or any of them.

Before he enter on the Execution of his Office, he shall take the following Oath or Affirmation:—"I do solemnly swear (or affirm) that I will faithfully execute the Office of President of the United States, and will to the best of my Ability, preserve, protect and defend the Constitution of the United States."

Section 2. The President shall be Commander in Chief of the Army and Navy of the United States, and of the Militia of the several States, when called into the actual Service of the United States; he may require the Opinion, in writing, of the principal Officer in each of the executive Departments, upon any Subject relating to the Duties of their respective Offices, and he shall have Power to grant Reprieves and Pardons for Offenses against the United States, except in Cases of Impeachment.

He shall have Power, by and with the Advice and Consent of the Senate, to make Treaties, provided two thirds of the Senators present concur; and he shall nominate, and by and with the Advice and Consent of the Senate, shall appoint Ambassadors, other public Ministers and Consuls, Judges of the supreme Court, and all other Officers of the United States, whose Appointments are not herein otherwise provided for, and which shall be established by Law: but the Congress may by Law vest the Appointment of such inferior Officers, as they think proper, in the President alone, in the Courts of Law, or in the Heads of Departments.

The President shall have Power to fill up all Vacancies that may happen during the Recess of the Senate, by granting Commissions which shall expire at the End of their next Session.

[7] Superseded by the Twenty-fifth Amendment.

Section 3. He shall from time to time give to the Congress Information of the State of the Union, and recommend to their Consideration such Measures as he shall judge necessary and expedient; he may, on extraordinary Occasions, convene both Houses, or either of them, and in Case of Disagreement between them, with Respect to the Time of Adjournment, he may adjourn them to such Time as he shall think proper; he shall receive Ambassadors and other public Ministers; he shall take Care that the Laws be faithfully executed, and shall Commission all Officers of the United States.

Section 4. The President, Vice President and all civil Officers of the United States, shall be removed from Office on Impeachment for, and Conviction of, Treason, Bribery, or other high Crimes and Misdemeanors.

ARTICLE III

Section 1. The judicial Power of the United States, shall be vested in one supreme Court, and in such inferior Courts as the Congress may from time to time ordain and establish. The Judges, both of the supreme and inferior Courts, shall hold their Offices during good Behaviour, and shall, at stated Times, receive for their Services, a Compensation, which shall not be diminished during their Continuance in Office.

Section 2. The judicial Power shall extend to all Cases, in Law and Equity, arising under this Constitution, the Laws of the United States, and Treaties made, or which shall be made, under their Authority;—to all Cases affecting Ambassadors, other public Ministers and Consuls;—to all Cases of admiralty and maritime Jurisdiction;—to Controversies to which the United States shall be a Party;—to Controversies between two or more States;—between a State and Citizens of another State;[7]—between Citizens of different States,—between Citizens of the same State claiming Lands under Grants of different States, and between a State, or the Citizens thereof, and foreign States, Citizens or Subjects.

In all cases affecting Ambassadors, other public Ministers and Consuls, and those in which a State shall be Party, the supreme Court shall have original Jurisdiction. In all the other Cases before mentioned, the supreme Court shall have appellate Juris-

[7] Modified by the Eleventh Amendment.

diction, both as to Law and fact, with such Exceptions, and under such Regulations as the Congress shall make.

The Trial of all Crimes, except in Cases of Impeachment, shall be by Jury; and such Trial shall be held in the State where the said Crimes shall have been committed; but when not committed within any State, the Trial shall be at such Place or Places as the Congress may by Law have directed.

Section 3. Treason against the United States, shall consist only in levying War against them, or in adhering to their Enemies, giving them Aid and Comfort. No Person shall be convicted of Treason unless on the Testimony of two Witnesses to the same overt Act, or on Confession in open Court.

The Congress shall have Power to declare the Punishment of Treason, but no Attainder of Treason shall work Corruption of Blood, or Forfeiture except during the Life of the Person attainted.

ARTICLE IV

Section 1. Full Faith and Credit shall be given in each State to the public Acts, Records, and judicial Proceedings of every other State. And the Congress may by general Laws prescribe the Manner in which such Acts, Records and Proceedings shall be proved, and the Effect thereof.

Section 2. The Citizens of each State shall be entitled to all Privileges and Immunities of Citizens in the several States.

A Person charged in any State with Treason, Felony, or other Crime, who shall flee from Justice, and be found in another State, shall on Demand of the executive Authority of the State from which he fled, be delivered up, to be removed to the State having Jurisdiction of the Crime.

No Person held to Service or Labour in one State, under the Laws thereof, escaping into another, shall in Consequence of any Law or Regulation therein, be discharged from such Service or Labour, but shall be delivered up on Claim of the Party to whom such Service or Labour may be due.

Section 3. New States may be admitted by the Congress into this Union; but no new State shall be formed or erected within the Jurisdiction of any other State; nor any State be formed by the Junction of two or more States, or Parts of States, without the Consent of the Legislatures of the States concerned as well as of the Congress.

The Congress shall have Power to dispose of and make all needful Rules and Regulations respecting the Territory or other Property belonging to the United States; and nothing in this Constitution shall be so construed as to Prejudice any Claims of the United States, or of any particular State.

Section 4. The United States shall guarantee to every State in this Union a Republican Form of Government, and shall protect each of them against Invasion; and on Application of the Legislature, or of the Executive (when the Legislature cannot be convened) against domestic Violence.

ARTICLE V

The Congress, whenever two thirds of both Houses shall deem it necessary, shall propose Amendments to this Constitution, or, on the Application of the Legislatures of two thirds of the several States, shall call a Convention for proposing Amendments, which, in either Case, shall be valid to all Intents and Purposes, as Part of this Constitution, when ratified by the Legislatures of three fourths of the several States, or by Conventions in three fourths thereof, as the one or the other Mode of Ratification may be proposed by the Congress; Provided that no Amendment which may be made prior to the Year One thousand eight hundred and eight shall in any Manner affect the first and fourth Clauses in the Ninth Section of the first Article; and that no State, without its Consent, shall be deprived of its equal Suffrage in the Senate.

ARTICLE VI

All Debts contracted and Engagements entered into, before the Adoption of this Constitution, shall be as valid against the United States under this Constitution, as under the Confederation.

This Constitution, and the Laws of the United States which shall be made in Pursuance thereof; and all Treaties made, or which shall be made, under the Authority of the United States, shall be the supreme Law of the Land; and the Judges in every

State shall be bound thereby, any Thing in the Constitution or Laws of any State to the Contrary notwithstanding.

The Senators and Representatives before mentioned, and the Members of the several State Legislatures, and all executive and judicial Officers, both of the United States and of the several States, shall be bound by Oath or Affirmation, to support this Constitution; but no religious Test shall ever be required as a Qualification to any Office or public Trust under the United States.

ARTICLE VII

The Ratification of the Conventions of nine States, shall be sufficient for the Establishment of this Constitution between the States so ratifying the Same.

[Signatures omitted.]

Amendments

ARTICLES in addition to, and Amendment of the Constitution of the United States of America, proposed by Congress, and ratified by the Legislatures of the several States, pursuant to the fifth Article of the original Constitution.

ARTICLE I

Congress shall make no law respecting an establishment of religion, or prohibiting the free exercise thereof; or abridging the freedom of speech, or of the press; or the right of the people peaceably to assemble, and to petition the Government for a redress of grievances.

ARTICLE II

A well regulated Militia, being necessary to the security of a free State, the right of the people to keep and bear Arms, shall not be infringed.

ARTICLE III

No Soldier shall, in time of peace, be quartered in any house, without the consent of the Owner, nor in time of war, but in a manner to be prescribed by law.

ARTICLE IV

The right of the people to be secure in their persons, houses, papers, and effects, against unreasonable searches and seizures, shall not be violated, and no Warrants shall issue, but upon probable cause, supported by Oath or affirmation, and particularly describing the place to be searched, and the persons or things to be seized.

ARTICLE V

No person shall be held to answer for a capital, or otherwise infamous crime, unless on a presentment or indictment of a Grand Jury, except in cases arising in the land or naval forces, or in the Militia, when in actual service in time of War or public danger; nor shall any person be subject for the same offense to be twice put in jeopardy of life or limb; nor shall be compelled in any criminal case to be a witness against himself, nor be deprived of life, liberty, or property, without due process of law; nor shall private property be taken for public use, without just compensation.

ARTICLE VI

In all criminal prosecutions, the accused shall enjoy the right to a speedy and public trial, by an impartial jury of the State and district wherein the crime shall have been committed, which district shall have been previously ascertained by law, and to be informed of the nature and cause of the accusation; to be confronted with the witnesses against him; to have compulsory process for obtaining witnesses in his favor, and to have the Assistance of Counsel for his defense.

ARTICLE VII

In Suits at common law, where the value in controversy shall exceed twenty dollars, the right of trial by jury shall be preserved, and no fact tried by a jury, shall be otherwise re-examined in any Court of the United States, than according to the rules of the common law.

ARTICLE VIII

Excessive bail shall not be required, nor excessive fines imposed, nor cruel and unusual punishments inflicted.

ARTICLE IX

The enumeration in the Constitution, of certain rights, shall not be construed to deny or disparage others retained by the people.

ARTICLE X

The powers not delegated to the United States by the Constitution, nor prohibited by it to the States, are reserved to the States respectively, or to the people.

ARTICLE XI [adopted in 1798]

The Judicial power of the United States shall not be construed to extend to any suit in law or equity, commenced or prosecuted against one of the United States by Citizens of another State, or by Citizens or Subjects of any Foreign State.

ARTICLE XII [adopted in 1804]

The Electors shall meet in their respective states, and vote by ballot for President and Vice-President, one of whom, at least, shall not be an inhabitant of the same state with themselves; they shall name in their ballots the person voted for as President, and in distinct ballots the person voted for as Vice-President, and they shall make distinct lists of all persons voted for as President, and of all persons voted for as Vice-President, and of the number of votes for each, which lists they shall sign and certify, and transmit sealed to the seat of the government of the United States, directed to the President of the Senate;—The President of the Senate shall, in the presence of the Senate and House of Representatives, open all certificates and the votes shall then be counted;—The person having the greatest number of votes for President, shall be the President, if such number be a majority of the whole number of Electors appointed; and if no person have such majority, then from the persons having the highest numbers not exceeding three on the list of those voted for as President, the House of Representatives shall choose immediately, by ballot, the President. But in choosing the President, the votes shall be taken by states, the representation from each state having one vote; a quorum for this purpose shall consist of a member or members from two-thirds of the states, and a majority of all the states shall be necessary to a choice. And if the House of Representatives shall not choose a President whenever the right of choice shall devolve upon them, before the fourth day of March next following, then the Vice-President shall act as President, as in the case of the death or other constitutional disability of the President.—The person having the greatest number of votes as Vice-President, shall be the Vice-President, if such number be a majority of the whole number of Electors appointed, and if no person have a majority, then from the two highest numbers on the list, the Senate shall choose the Vice-President; a quorum for the purpose shall consist of two-thirds of the whole number of Senators, and a majority of the whole number shall be necessary to a choice. But no person constitutionally ineligible to the office of President shall be eligible to that of Vice-President of the United States.

ARTICLE XIII [adopted in 1865]

Section 1. Neither slavery nor involuntary servitude, except as a punishment for crime whereof the party shall have been duly convicted, shall exist within the United States, or any place subject to their jurisdiction.

Section 2. Congress shall have power to enforce this article by appropriate legislation.

ARTICLE XIV [adopted in 1868]

Section 1. All persons born or naturalized in the United States, and subject to the jurisdiction thereof, are citizens of the United

States and of the State wherein they reside. No State shall make or enforce any law which shall abridge the privileges or immunities of citizens of the United States; nor shall any State deprive any person of life, liberty, or property, without due process of law; nor deny to any person within its jurisdiction the equal protection of the laws.

Section 2. Representatives shall be apportioned among the several States according to their respective numbers, counting the whole number of persons in each State, excluding Indians not taxed. But when the right to vote at any election for the choice of electors for President and Vice President of the United States, Representatives in Congress, the Executive and Judicial officers of a State, or the members of the Legislature thereof, is denied to any of the male inhabitants of such State, being twenty-one years of age, and citizens of the United States, or in any way abridged, except for participation in rebellion, or other crime, the basis of representation therein shall be reduced in the proportion which the number of such male citizens shall bear to the whole number of male citizens twenty-one years of age in such State.

Section 3. No person shall be a Senator or Representative in Congress, or elector of President and Vice President, or hold any office, civil or military, under the United States, or under any State, who, having previously taken an oath, as a member of Congress, or as an officer of the United States, or as a member of any State legislature, or as an executive or judicial officer of any States, to support the Constitution of the United States, shall have engaged in insurrection or rebellion against the same, or given aid and comfort to the enemies thereof. But Congress may by a vote of two-thirds of each House, remove such disability.

Section 4. The validity of the public debt of the United States, authorized by law, including debts incurred for payment of pensions and bounties for services in suppressing insurrection or rebellion, shall not be questioned. But neither the United States nor any state shall assume or pay any debt or obligation incurred in aid of insurrection or rebellion against the United States, or any claim for the loss or emancipation of any slave; but all such debts, obligations, and claims shall be held illegal and void.

Section 5. The Congress shall have power to enforce, by appropriate legislation, the provisions of this article.

ARTICLE XV [proclaimed 30 Mar. 1870]

Section 1. The right of citizens of the United States to vote shall not be denied or abridged by the United States or by any State on account of race, color, or previous condition of servitude.

Section 2. The Congress shall have power to enforce this article by appropriate legislation.

ARTICLE XVI [proclaimed 25 Feb. 1913]

The Congress shall have power to lay and collect taxes on incomes, from whatever source derived, without apportionment among the several States, and without regard to any census or enumeration.

ARTICLE XVII [proclaimed 31 May 1913]

The Senate of the United States shall be composed of two Senators from each State, elected by the people thereof, for six years; and each Senator shall have one vote. The electors in each State shall have the qualifications requisite for electors of the most numerous branch of the State legislatures.

When vacancies happen in the representation of any State in the Senate, the executive authority of such State shall issue writs of election to fill such vacancies: *Provided,* That the legislature of any State may empower the executive thereof to make temporary appointments until the people fill the vacancies by election as the legislature may direct.

This amendment shall not be so construed as to affect the election or term of any Senator chosen before it becomes valid as part of the Constitution.

ARTICLE XVIII [proclaimed 29 Jan. 1919; repealed by the 21st Amendment]

Section 1. After one year from the ratification of this article the manufacture, sale, or transportation of intoxicating liquors within, the importation thereof into, or the exportation thereof from the United States and all territory subject to the jurisdiction thereof for beverage purposes is hereby prohibited.

Section 2. The Congress and the several States shall have concurrent power to enforce this article by appropriate legislation.

Section 3. This article shall be inoperative unless it shall have been ratified as an amendment to the Constitution by the legislatures of the several States, as provided in the Constitution, within seven years from the date of the submission thereof to the States by the Congress.

ARTICLE XIX [adopted in 1920]

The right of citizens of the United States to vote shall not be denied or abridged by the United States or by any State on account of sex.

Congress shall have power to enforce this article by appropriate legislation.

ARTICLE XX [adopted in 1933]

Section 1. The terms of the President and Vice President shall end at noon on the 20th day of January, and the terms of Senators and Representatives at noon on the 3d day of January, of the years in which such terms would have ended if this article had not been ratified; and the terms of their successors shall then begin.

Section 2. The Congress shall assemble at least once in every year, and such meeting shall begin at noon on the 3d day of January, unless they shall by law appoint a different day.

Section 3. If, at the time fixed for the beginning of the term of the President, the President elect shall have died, the Vice President elect shall become President. If a President shall not have been chosen before the time fixed for the beginning of his term, or if the President elect shall have failed to qualify, then the Vice President elect shall act as President until a President shall have qualified; and the Congress may by law provide for the case wherein neither a President elect nor a Vice President elect shall have qualified, declaring who shall then act as President, or the manner in which one who is to act shall be selected, and such person shall act accordingly until a President or Vice President shall have qualified.

Section 4. The Congress may by law provide for the case of the death of any of the persons from whom the House of Representatives may choose a President whenever the right of choice shall have devolved upon them, and for the case of the death of any of the persons from whom the Senate may choose a Vice President whenever the right of choice shall have devolved upon them.

Section 5. Sections 1 and 2 shall take effect on the 15th day of October following the ratification of this article.

Section 6. This article shall be inoperative unless it shall have been ratified as an amendment to the Constitution by the legislatures of three-fourths of the several States within seven years from the date of its submission.

ARTICLE XXI [adopted in 1933]

Section 1. The Eighteenth article of amendment to the Constitution of the United States is hereby repealed.

Section 2. The transportation or importation into any State, Territory, or possession of the United States for delivery or use therein of intoxicating liquors, in violation of the laws thereof, is hereby prohibited.

Section 3. This article shall be inoperative unless it shall have been ratified as an amendment to the Constitution by conventions in the several States, as provided in the Constitution, within seven years from the date of the submission hereof to the States by the Congress.

ARTICLE XXII [adopted in 1951]

Section 1. No person shall be elected to the office of the President more than twice, and no person who has held the office of President, or acted as President, for more than two years of a term to which some other person was elected President shall be elected to the office of the President more than once. But this

Article shall not apply to any person holding the office of President when this Article was proposed by the Congress, and shall not prevent any person who may be holding the office of President, or acting as President, during the term within which this Article becomes operative from holding the office of President or acting as President during the remainder of such term.

Section 2. This article shall be inoperative unless it shall have been ratified as an amendment to the Constitution by the legislatures of three-fourths of the several States within seven years from the date of its submission to the States by the Congress.

Amendment XXIII [adopted in 1961]

Section 1. The District constituting the seat of Government of the United States shall appoint in such manner as the Congress may direct:

A number of electors of President and Vice President equal to the whole number of Senators and Representatives in Congress to which the District would be entitled if it were a State, but in no event more than the least populous State; they shall be in addition to those appointed by the States, but they shall be considered, for the purposes of the election of President and Vice President, to be electors appointed by a State; and they shall meet in the District and perform such duties as provided by the twelfth article of amendment.

Section 2. The Congress shall have power to enforce this article by appropriate legislation.

Amendment XXIV [adopted in 1964]

Section 1. The right of citizens of the United States to vote in any primary or other election for President or Vice President, for electors for President or Vice President, or for Senator or Representative in Congress, shall not be denied or abridged by the United States or any State by reason of failure to pay any poll tax or other tax.

Section 2. The Congress shall have power to enforce this article by appropriate legislation.

AMENDMENT XXV [adopted in 1967]

Section 1. In case of the removal of the President from office or of his death or resignation, the Vice President shall become President.

Section 2. Whenever there is a vacancy in the office of the Vice President, the President shall nominate a Vice President who shall take office upon confirmation by a majority vote of both Houses of Congress.

Section 3. Whenever the President transmits to the President pro tempore of the Senate and the Speaker of the House of Representatives his written declaration that he is unable to discharge the powers and duties of his office, and until he transmits to them a written declaration to the contrary, such powers and duties shall be discharged by the Vice President as Acting President.

Section 4. Whenever the Vice President and a majority of either the principal officers of the executive departments or of such other body as Congress may by law provide, transmit to the President pro tempore of the Senate and the Speaker of the House of Representatives their written declaration that the President is unable to discharge the powers and duties of his office, the Vice President shall immediately assume the powers and duties of the office as Acting President.

Thereafter, when the President transmits to the President pro tempore of the Senate and the Speaker of the House of Representatives his written declaration that no inability exists, he shall resume the powers and duties of his office unless the Vice President and a majority of either the principal officers of the executive department or of such other body as Congress may by law provide, transmit within four days to the President pro tempore of the Senate and the Speaker of the House of Representatives their written declaration that the President is unable to discharge the powers and duties of his office. Thereupon Congress shall decide the issue, assembling within forty-eight hours for that purpose if not in session. If the Congress, within twenty-one days after receipt of the latter written declaration, or, if Congress is not in session, within twenty-one days after Congress is required to assemble, determines by two-thirds vote of both Houses that the President is unable to discharge the powers and duties of his office, the Vice President shall continue to discharge the same as Acting President; otherwise, the President shall resume the powers and duties of his office.

Chapter XIII

FEDERALISTS VS. ANTIFEDERALISTS

Among the most influential opponents of the new Constitution were two prominent Virginians, George Mason and Richard Henry Lee. Mason stressed the omission of a bill of rights as a major ground for opposing ratification as well as the large powers conferred upon the judiciary and the executive. Writing under the pseudonym of "A Federal Farmer," Lee stressed as short-comings of the proposed Constitution the failure to have a bill of rights, the lack of full and equal representation, and the re-moteness of the central government from the people.

When, in October 1787, Alexander Hamilton, James Madison, and John Jay launched a series of articles to help secure ratifica-tion of the new Constitution, it could hardly have been foreseen that this set of eighty-five papers would prove to be the most comprehensive marshaling of arguments in support of the Con-stitution and would be accepted almost at once as a classic analy-sis of federalism. The first Federalist paper, written by Alexander Hamilton, provides an excellent introduction to the nature of the problems and outlines the subjects to be covered in future arti-cles.

Of the eighty-five Federalist letters, perhaps the tenth is best known and seems to have a special relevance to our own age. Therein James Madison argued the case for a strong union under a republican form of government "to break and control the vio-lence of faction." Recognizing the various interest groups that make up society, Madison saw the most common cause of fac-tion to be grounded in the unequal distribution of property.

Along with the favorable opinions of the Constitution enun-ciated by erudite writers were those of common unlettered farm-ers like Jonathan Smith of Massachusetts. Smith, a delegate from Bristol County to the Massachusetts ratifying convention, viewed the new Constitution as a cure for the anarchy that existed. He

*saw no conflict between a man who owned fifty acres and one
who possessed 5,000. "These lawyers, these moneyed men, these
men of learning," he said, "are all embarked in the same cause
with us, and we must all swim or sink together."*

46.   George Mason's Objection to the Proposed Constitution, October, 1787 *

There is no declaration of rights; and, the laws of the general
government being paramount to the laws and constitutions of
the several states, the declarations of rights in the separate states
are no security. Nor are the people secured even in the enjoyment of the benefit of the common law, which stands here upon
no other foundation than its having been adopted by the respective acts forming the constitutions of the several states.

In the House of Representatives there is not the substance, but
the shadow only, of representation, which can never produce
proper information in the legislature, or inspire confidence in
the people. The laws will, therefore, be generally made by men
little concerned in, and unacquainted with, their effects and consequences.

The Senate have the power of altering all money bills, and of
originating appropriations of money, and the salaries of the
officers of their own appointment, in conjunction with the President of the United States, although they are not the representatives of the people, or amenable to them. These, with their other
great powers, (viz., their powers in the appointment of ambas-

* P. F. Ford (ed.), *Pamphlets on the Constitution of the United States,
Published During Its Discussion by the People, 1787–1788* (Brook-
lyn, N.Y., 1888), 327–332.

sadors, and all public officers, in making treaties, and in trying all impeachments;) their influence upon, and connection with, the supreme executive from these causes; their duration of office; and their being a constant existing body, almost continually sitting, joined with their being one complete branch of the legislature,—will destroy any balance in the government, and enable them to accomplish what usurpations they please upon the rights and liberties of the people.

The judiciary of the United States is so constructed and extended as to absorb and destroy the judiciaries of the several states; thereby rendering laws as tedious, intricate, and expensive, and justice as unattainable, by a great part of the community, as in England; and enabling the rich to oppress and ruin the poor.

The President of the United States has no constitutional council, (a thing unknown in any safe and regular government.) He will therefore be unsupported by proper information and advice, and will generally be directed by minions and favorites; or he will become a tool to the Senate; or a council of state will grow out of the principal officers of the great departments—the worst and most dangerous of all ingredients for such a council, in a free country; for they may be induced to join in any dangerous or oppressive measures, to shelter themselves, and prevent an inquiry into their own misconduct in office. Whereas, had a constitutional council been formed (as was proposed) of six members, viz., two from the Eastern, two from the Middle, and two from the Southern States, to be appointed by vote of the states in the House of Representatives, with the same duration and rotation of office as the Senate, the executive would always have had safe and proper information and advice: the president of such a council might have acted as Vice-President of the United States, *pro tempore,* upon any vacancy or disability of the chief magistrate; and long-continued sessions of the Senate would in a great measure have been prevented. From this fatal defect of a constitutional council has arisen the improper power of the Senate in the appointment of the public officers, and the alarming dependence and connection between that branch of the legislature and the supreme executive. Hence, also, sprang that unnecessary officer, the Vice-President, who, for want of other employment, is made president of the Senate; thereby dangerously blending the executive and legislative powers, besides always giving to some one of the states an unnecessary and unjust preëminence over the others.

The President of the United States has the unrestrained power of granting pardon for treason; which may be sometimes exercised to screen from punishment those whom he had secretly instigated to commit the crime, and thereby prevent a discovery of his own guilt. By declaring all treaties supreme laws of the land, the executive and the Senate have, in many cases, an exclusive power of legislation, which might have been avoided, by proper distinctions with respect to treaties, and requiring the assent of the House of Representatives, where it could be done with safety.

By requiring only a majority to make all commercial and navigation laws, the five Southern States (whose produce and circumstances are totally different from those of the eight Northern and Eastern States) will be ruined; for such rigid and premature regulations may be made, as will enable the merchants of the Northern and Eastern States not only to demand an exorbitant freight, but to monopolize the purchase of the commodities, at their own price, for many years, to the great injury of the landed interest, and the impoverishment of the people; and the danger is the greater, as the gain on one side will be in proportion to the loss on the other. Whereas, requiring two thirds of the members present in both houses, would have produced mutual moderation, promoted the general interest, and removed an insuperable objection to the adoption of the government.

Under their own construction of the general clause at the end of the enumerated powers, the Congress may grant monopolies in trade and commerce, constitute new crimes, inflict unusual and severe punishments, and extend their power as far as they shall think proper; so that the state legislatures have no security for the powers now presumed to remain to them, or the people for their rights. There is no declaration of any kind for preserving the liberty of the press, the trial by jury in civil cases, nor against the danger of standing armies in time of peace.

The state legislatures are restrained from laying export duties on their own produce; the general legislature is restrained from prohibiting the further importation of slaves for twenty-odd years, though such importations render the United States weaker, more vulnerable, and less capable of defence. Both the general legislature and the state legislatures are expressly prohibited making *ex post facto* laws, though there never was, nor can be, a legislature but must and will make such laws, when necessity and the public safety require them, which will hereafter be a breach of all the constitutions in the Union, and afford precedents for other innovations.

This government will commence in a moderate aristocracy: it is at present impossible to foresee whether it will, in its operation, produce a monarchy or a corrupt oppressive aristocracy; it will most probably vibrate some years between the two, and then terminate in the one or the other.

GEO. MASON

47. Richard Henry Lee's "Letters of the Federal Farmer," October 9 and 10, 1787 *

Letter II

9 October 1787

Dear Sir,

The essential parts of a free and good government are a full and equal representation of the people in the legislature, and the jury trial of the vicinage in the administration of justice—a full and equal representation, is that which possesses the same interests, feelings, opinions, and views the people themselves would

* P. F. Ford, ed., *Pamphlets on the Constitution of the United States, 1787–1788,* 288–293, 294–299.

were they all assembled—a fair representation, therefore, should be so regulated, that every order of men in the community, according to the common course of elections, can have a share in it—in order to allow professional men, merchants, traders, farmers, mechanics, &c. to bring a just proportion of their best informed men respectively into the legislature, the representation must be considerably numerous—We have about 200 state senators in the United States, and a less number than that of federal representatives cannot, clearly, be a full representation of this people, in the affairs of internal taxation and police, were there but one legislature for the whole union. The representation cannot be equal, or the situation of the people proper for one government only—if the extreme parts of the society cannot be represented as fully as the central—It is apparently impracticable that this should be the case in this extensive country—it would be impossible to collect a representation of the parts of the country five, six, and seven hundred miles from the seat of government.

Under one general government alone, there could be but one judiciary, one supreme and a proper number of inferior courts. I think it would be totally impracticable in this case to preserve a due administration of justice, and the real benefits of the jury trial of the vicinage—there are now supreme courts in each state in the union, and a great number of county and other courts subordinate to each supreme court—most of these supreme and inferior courts are itinerant, and hold their sessions in different parts every year of their respective states, counties and districts —with all these moving courts, our citizens, from the vast extent of the country, must travel very considerable distances from home to find the place where justice is administered. . . .

If it were possible to consolidate the states, and preserve the features of a free government, still it is evident that the middle states, the parts of the union, about the seat of government, would enjoy great advantages, while the remote states would experience the many inconveniences of remote provinces. Wealth, offices, and the benefits of government would collect in the centre: and the extreme states; and their principal towns, become much less important.

There are other considerations which tend to prove that the idea of one consolidated whole, on free principles, is ill-founded —the laws of a free government rest on the confidence of the people, and operate gently—and never can extend the influence very far—if they are executed on free principles, about the centre, where the benefits of the government induce the people to support it voluntarily; yet they must be executed on the principles of fear and force in the extremes—This has been the case with every extensive republic of which we have any accurate account.

There are certain unalienable and fundamental rights, which in forming the social compact, ought to be explicitly ascertained and fixed—a free and enlightened people, in forming this compact, will not resign all their rights to those who govern, and they will fix limits to their legislators and rulers . . . . These rights should be made the basis of every constitution; and if a people be so situated, or have such different opinions that they cannot agree in ascertaining and fixing them, it is a very strong argument against their attempting to form one entire society, to live under one system of laws only.—I confess, I never thought the people of these states differed essentially in these respects; they having derived all these rights from one common source, the British systems; and having in the formation of their state constitutions, discovered that their ideas relative to these rights are very similar. However, it is now said that the states differ so essentially in these respects, and even in the important article of the trial by jury, that when assembled in convention, they can agree to no words by which to establish that trial . . . . If so, we proceed to consolidate the states on no solid basis whatever.

But I do not pay much regard to the reasons given for not bottoming the new constitution on a better bill of rights. I still believe a complete federal bill of rights to be very practicable. . . .

In examining the proposed constitution carefully, we must clearly perceive an unnatural separation of these powers from the substantial representation of the people. The state governments will exist, with all their governors, senators, representatives, officers and expences; in these will be nineteen twentieths of the representatives of the people; they will have a near connection, and their members an immediate intercourse with the people; and the probability is, that the state governments will possess the confidence of the people, and be considered generally as their immediate guardians.

The general government will consist of a new species of executive, a small senate, and a very small house of representatives. As many citizens will be more than three hundred miles from the seat of this government as will be nearer to it, its judges and officers cannot be very numerous, without making our governments very expensive. Thus will stand the state and the general governments, should the constitution be adopted without any alterations in their organization; but as to powers, the general government will possess all essential ones, at least on paper, and those of the states a mere shadow of power. And therefore, unless the people shall make some great exertions to restore to the state governments their powers in matters of internal police; as the powers to lay and collect, exclusively, internal taxes, to govern the militia, and to hold the decisions of their own judicial courts upon their own laws final, the balance cannot possibly continue long; but the state governments must be annihilated, or continue to exist for no purpose.

. . . The powers lodged in the general government, if exercised by it, must intimately effect the internal police of the states, as well as external concerns; and there is no reason to expect the numerous state governments, and their connections, will be very friendly to the execution of federal laws in those internal affairs, which hitherto have been under their own immediate management. There is more reason to believe, that the general government, far removed from the people, and none of its members elected oftener than once in two years, will be forgot or neglected, and its laws in many cases disregarded, unless a multitude of officers and military force be continually kept in view, and employed to enforce the execution of the laws, and to make the government feared and respected. . . . Neglected laws must first lead to anarchy and confusion; and a military execution of laws is only a shorter way to the same point—despotic government.

Your's, &c.
THE FEDERAL FARMER

Letter III

10 October 1787

Dear Sir,

*   *   *   *   *   *   *

First. As to the organization—the house of representatives, the democratic branch, as it is called, is to consist of 65 members: that is, about one representative for fifty thousand inhabitants, to be chosen biennially . . . . I have no idea that the interests, feelings, and opinions of three or four millions of people, especially touching internal taxation, can be collected in such a house.—In the nature of things, nine times in ten, men of the elevated classes in the community only can be chosen—Connecticut, for instance, will have five representatives—not one man in a hundred of those who form the democrative branch in the state legislature, will, on a fair computation, be one of the five. —The people of this country, in one sense, may all be democratic; but if we make the proper distinction between the few men of wealth and abilities, and consider them, as we ought, as the natural aristocracy of the country, and the great body of the people, the middle and lower classes, as the democracy, this federal representative branch will have but very little democracy in it . . . .

In considering the practicability of having a full and equal representation of the people from all parts of the union, not only distances and different opinions, customs and views, common in extensive tracts of country, are to be taken into view, but many differences peculiar to Eastern, Middle, and Southern States. . . . The Eastern states are very democratic, and composed chiefly of moderate freeholders; they have but few rich men and no slaves; the Southern states are composed chiefly of rich planters and slaves; they have but few moderate freeholders, and the prevailing influence, in them is generally a dissipated aristocracy: The Middle states partake partly of the Eastern and partly of the Southern character. . . .

The house of representatives is on the plan of consolidation, but the senate is entirely on the federal plan; and Delaware will have as much constitutional influence in the senate, as the largest state in the union . . . . I suppose it was impracticable for the three large states, as they were called, to get the senate formed on any other principles: But this only proves, that we cannot form one general government on equal and just principles—and proves, that we ought not to lodge in it such extensive powers before we are convinced of the practicability of organizing it on just and equal principles. . . .

. . . [When] we examine the powers of the president, and the forms of the executive, we shall perceive that the general government, in this part, will have a strong tendency to aristocracy, or the government of the few. . . .

. . . The plan does not present a well balanced government: The senatorial branch of the legislative and the executive are substantially united, and the president, or the state executive magistrate, may aid the senatorial interest when weakest, but never can effectually support the democratic, however it may be opposed . . . .

Your's, &c.

THE FEDERAL FARMER

48.   Alexander Hamilton's *Federalist* Essay No. 1, October 27, 1787 *

To the People of the State of New York:

After an unequivocal experience of the inefficiency of the subsisting federal government, you are called upon to deliberate on a new Constitution for the United States of America. The sub-

* John C. Hamilton (ed.), *Federalist* (Philadelphia, 1864), 49–53.

ject speaks its own importance; comprehending in its consequences nothing less than the existence of the UNION, the safety and welfare of the parts of which it is composed, the fate of an empire in many respects the most interesting in the world. It has been frequently remarked that it seems to have been reserved to the people of this country, by their conduct and example, to decide the important question, whether societies of men are really capable or not of establishing good government from reflection and choice, or whether they are forever destined to depend for their political constitutions on accident and force. If there be any truth in the remark, the crisis at which we are arrived may with propriety be regarded as the era in which that decision is to be made; and a wrong election of the part we shall act may, in this view, deserve to be considered as the general misfortune of mankind.

This idea will add the inducements of philanthropy to those of patriotism, to heighten the solicitude which all considerate and good men must feel for the event. Happy will it be if our choice should be directed by a judicious estimate of our true interests, unperplexed and unbiased by considerations not connected with the public good. But this is a thing more ardently to be wished than seriously to be expected. The plan offered to our deliberations affects too many particular interests, innovates upon too many local institutions, not to involve in its discussion a variety of objects foreign to its merits, and of views, passions, and prejudices little favorable to the discovery of truth.

Among the most formidable of the obstacles which the new Constitution will have to encounter may readily be distinguished the obvious interest of a certain class of men in every State to resist all changes which may hazard a diminution of the power, emolument, and consequence of the offices they hold under the State establishment; and the perverted ambition of another class of men, who will either hope to aggrandize themselves by the confusions of their country, or will flatter themselves with fairer prospects of elevation from the subdivision of the empire into several partial confederacies than from its union under one government.

It is not, however, my design to dwell upon observations of this nature. I am well aware that it would be disingenuous to resolve indiscriminately the opposition of any set of men (merely because their situations might subject them to suspicion) into interested or ambitious views. Candor will oblige us to admit that even such men may be actuated by upright intentions; and it cannot be doubted that much of the opposition which has made its appearance, or may hereafter make its appearance, will spring from sources, blameless, at least, if not respectable—the honest errors of minds led astray by preconceived jealousies and fears. So numerous indeed and so powerful are the causes which serve to give a false bias to the judgment, that we, upon many occasions, see wise and good men on the wrong as well as on the right side of questions of the first magnitude to society. This circumstance, if duly attended to, would furnish a lesson of moderation to those who are ever so much persuaded of their being in the right in any controversy. And a further reason for caution, in this respect, might be drawn from the reflection that we are not always sure that those who advocate the truth are influenced by purer principles than their antagonists. Ambition, avarice, personal animosity, party opposition, and many other motives not more laudable than these, are apt to operate as well upon those who support as those who oppose the right side of a question. Were there not even these inducements to moderation, nothing could be more ill-judged than that intolerant spirit which has, at all times, characterized political parties. For in politics, as in religion, it is equally absurd to aim at making proselytes by fire and sword. Heresies in either can rarely be cured by persecution.

And yet, however just these sentiments will be allowed to be, we have already sufficient indications that it will happen in this as in all former cases of great national discussion. A torrent of angry and malignant passions will be let loose. To judge from the conduct of the opposite parties, we shall be led to conclude that they will mutually hope to evince the justness of their opinions, and to increase the number of their converts by the loudness of their declamations and the bitterness of their invectives. An enlightened zeal for the energy and efficiency of government will be stigmatized as the offspring of a temper fond of despotic power and hostile to the principles of liberty. And overscrupulous jealousy of danger to the rights of the people, which is more commonly the fault of the head than of the heart, will be represented as mere pretense and artifice, the stale bait for popularity at the expense of the public good. It will be forgotten, on the other hand, that jealousy is the usual concomitant of love, and that the noble enthusiasm of liberty is apt to be infected with a spirit of narrow and illiberal distrust. On the other hand, it will be equally forgotten that the vigor of government is essential to the security of liberty; that, in the contemplation of a sound and well-informed judgment, their interest can never be separated; and that a dangerous ambition more often lurks behind the specious mask of zeal for the rights of the people than under the forbidding appearance of zeal for the firmness and efficiency of government. History will teach us that the former has been found a much more certain road to the introduction of despotism than the latter, and that of those men who have overturned the liberties of republics, the greatest number have begun their career by paying an obsequious court to the people; commencing demagogues, and ending tyrants.

In the course of the preceding observations, I have had an eye, my fellow-citizens, to putting you upon your guard against all attempts, from whatever quarter, to influence your decision in a matter of the utmost moment to your welfare, by any impressions other than those which may result from the evidence of truth. You will, no doubt, at the same time have collected from the general scope of them, that they proceed from a source not unfriendly to the new Constitution. Yes, my countrymen, I own to you that, after having given it an attentive consideration, I am clearly of opinion it is your interest to adopt it. I am convinced that this is the safest course for your liberty, your dignity, and your happiness. I affect not reserves which I do not feel. I will not amuse you with an appearance of deliberation when I have decided. I frankly acknowledge to you my convictions, and I will freely lay before you the reasons on which they are founded. The consciousness of good intentions disdains ambiguity. I shall not, however, multiply professions on this head. My motives must remain in the depository of my own breast. My arguments will be open to all, and may be judged of by all. They shall at least be offered in a spirit which will not disgrace the cause of truth.

I propose, in a series of papers, to discuss the following interesting particulars:—*The utility of the UNION to your political prosperity*—*The insufficiency of the present confederation to preserve that Union*—*the necessity of a government at least equally energetic with the one proposed, to the attainment of this object*—*The conformity of the proposed Constitution to the true principles of republican government*—*Its analogy to your own State constitution*—and lastly, *The additional security which its adoption will afford to the preservation of that species of government, to liberty, and to property.*

In the progress of this discussion I shall endeavor to give a satisfactory answer to all the objections which shall have made their appearance, that may seem to have any claim to your attention.

It may perhaps be thought superfluous to offer arguments to prove the utility of the UNION, a point, no doubt, deeply engraved on the hearts of the great body of the people in every State, and one which, it may be imagined, has no adversaries. But the fact is that we already hear it whispered in the private circles of those who oppose the new Constitution, that the thirteen States are of too great extent for any general system, and that we must of necessity resort to separate confederacies of distinct portions of the whole. This doctrine will, in all probability, be gradually propagated, till it has votaries enough to countenance an open avowal of it. For nothing can be more evident to those who are able to take an enlarged view of the subject than the alternative of an adoption of the new Constitution or a dismemberment of the Union. It will therefore be of use to begin by examining the advantages of that Union, the certain evils, and the probable dangers, to which every State will be exposed from its dissolution. This shall accordingly constitute the subject of my next address.

PUBLIUS [HAMILTON]

49. James Madison's *Federalist* Essay No. 10, November 24, 1787 *

Among the numerous advantages promised by a well-constructed union, none deserves to be more accurately developed than its tendency to break and control the violence of faction. The friend of popular governments never finds himself so much alarmed for their character and fate as when he contemplates their propensity to this dangerous vice. He will not fail, therefore, to set a due value on any plan which, without violating the principles to which he is attached, provides a proper cure for it. . . . Complaints are everywhere heard from our most considerate and virtuous citizens, equally the friends of public and private faith and of public and personal liberty, that our governments are too unstable; that the public good is disregarded in the conflicts of rival parties; and that measures are too often decided, not according to the rules of justice and the rights of the minor party, but by the superior force of an interested and overbearing majority. . . . That prevailing and increasing distrust of public engagements, and alarm for private rights . . . must be chiefly, if not wholly, effects of the unsteadiness and injustice with which a factious spirit has tainted our public administrations.

By a faction, I understand a number of citizens, whether amounting to a majority or minority of the whole, who are united and actuated by some common impulse of passion, or of interest, adverse to the rights of other citizens or to the permanent and aggregate interests of the community.

* John C. Hamilton (ed.), *Federalist*, 104–112.

There are two methods of curing the mischiefs of faction: the one, by removing its causes, the other, by controlling its effects.

There are again two methods of removing the causes of faction: the one, by destroying the liberty which is essential to its existence; the other, by giving to every citizen the same opinions, the same passions, and the same interests.

It could never be more truly said than of the first remedy, that it was worse than the disease. . . .

The second expedient is as impracticable as the first would be unwise. As long as the reason of man continues fallible, and he is at liberty to exercise it, different opinions will be formed. As long as the connection subsists between his reason and his self-love, his opinions and his passions will have a reciprocal influence on each other; and the former will be objects to which the latter will attach themselves. The diversity in the faculties of men, from which the rights of property originate, is not less an insuperable obstacle to a uniformity of interests. . . .

The latent causes of faction are thus sown in the nature of man; and we see them everywhere brought into different degrees of activity, according to the different circumstances of civil society. . . . But the most common and durable source of factions has been the various and unequal distribution of property. Those who hold and those who are without property have ever formed distinct interests in society. Those who are creditors and those who are debtors fall under a like discrimination. A landed interest, a manufacturing interest, a mercantile interest, a moneyed interest, with many lesser interests, grow up of necessity in civilized nations, and divide them into different classes, actuated by different sentiments and views. The regulation of these various and interfering interests forms the principal task of modern legislation, and involves the spirit of party and faction in the necessary and ordinary operations of the government.

No man is allowed to be a judge in his own cause; because his interest would certainly bias his judgment and, not improbably, corrupt his integrity. With equal, nay, with greater reason, a body of men are unfit to be both judges and parties at the same time; yet what are many of the most important acts of legislation, but so many judicial determinations, not indeed concerning the rights of single persons, but concerning the rights of large bodies of citizens? And what are the different classes of legislators, but advocates and parties to the causes which they determine? . . .

It is in vain to say that enlightened statesmen will be able to adjust these clashing interests and render them all subservient to the public good. Enlightened statesmen will not always be at the helm. Nor, in many cases, can such an adjustment be made at all, without taking into view indirect and remote considerations, which will rarely prevail over the immediate interest which one party may find in disregarding the rights of another or the good of the whole.

The inference to which we are brought is that the causes of faction cannot be removed, and that relief is only to be sought in the means of controlling its effects.

If a faction consists of less than a majority, relief is supplied by the republican principle, which enables the majority to defeat its sinister views by regular vote. It may clog the administration, it may convulse the society; but it will be unable to execute and mask its violence under the forms of the Constitution. When a majority is included in a faction, the form of popular government, on the other hand, enables it to sacrifice to its ruling passion or interest both the public good and the rights of other citizens. To secure the public good and private rights against the danger of such a faction, and at the same time to preserve the spirit and the form of popular government, is then the great object to which our inquiries are directed. . . .

By what means is this object attainable? Evidently by one of two only. Either the existence of the same passion or interest in a majority, at the same time, must be prevented; or the majority, having such coexistent passion or interest, must be rendered, by their number and local situation, unable to concert and carry into effect schemes of oppression. If the impulse and the opportunity be suffered to coincide, we well know that neither moral nor religious motives can be relied on as an adequate control. They are not found to be such on the injustice and violence of individuals, and lose their efficacy in proportion to the number combined together; that is, in proportion as their efficacy becomes needful. . . .

A republic, by which I mean a government in which the scheme of representation takes place, opens a different prospect, and promises the cure for which we are seeking. Let us examine the points in which it varies from pure democracy, and we shall comprehend both the nature of the cure and the efficacy which it must derive from the union.

The two great points of difference between a democracy and a republic are: first, the delegation of the government, in the latter, to a small number of citizens elected by the rest; secondly, the greater number of citizens, and greater sphere of country, over which the latter may be extended.

The effect of the first difference is, on the one hand, to refine and enlarge the public views, by passing them through the medium of a chosen body of citizens, whose wisdom may best discern the true interest of their country, and whose patriotism and love of justice will be least likely to sacrifice it to temporary or partial considerations. Under such a regulation, it may well happen that the public voice, pronounced by the representatives of the people, will be more consonant to the public good than if pronounced by the people themselves, convened for the purpose. . . .

The other point of difference is, the greater number of citizens and extent of territory which may be brought within the compass of republican than of democratic government; and it is this circumstance principally which renders factions combinations less to be dreaded in the former, than in the latter. The smaller the society, the fewer probably will be the distinct parties and interests composing it; the fewer the distinct parties and interests, the more frequently will a majority be found of the same party; and the smaller the number of individuals composing a majority, and the smaller the compass within which they are placed, the more easily will they concert and execute their plans of oppression. Extend the sphere, and you take in a greater variety of parties and interests; you make it less probable that a majority of the whole will have a common motive to invade the rights of other citizens; or if such a common motive exists, it will be more difficult for all who feel it to discover their own strength, and to act in unison with each other. Besides other impediments, it may be remarked that where there is a consciousness of unjust or dishonorable purposes, communication is always checked by distrust, in proportion to the number whose concurrence is necessary.

Hence it clearly appears that the same advantage which a republic has over a democracy, in controlling the effects of faction,
is enjoyed by a large over a small republic—is enjoyed by the
Union over the States composing it.

50.   Jonathan Smith's Speech in the Massachusetts Ratifying Convention, January 25, 1788 *

Hon. Mr. SMITH. Mr. President, I am a plain man, and get
my living by the plough. I am not used to speak in public, but I
beg your leave to say a few words to my brother ploughjoggers
in this house. I have lived in a part of the country where I have
known the worth of good government by the want of it. There
was a black cloud that rose in the east last winter, and spread
over the west. [Here Mr. Widgery interrupted. Mr. President, I
wish to know what the gentleman means by the east.] I mean, sir,
the county of Bristol; the cloud rose there, and burst upon us,
and produced a dreadful effect. It brought on a state of anarchy,
and that led to tyranny. I say, it brought anarchy. People that
used to live peaceably, and were before good neighbors, got dis-
tracted, and took up arms against government. [Here Mr. King-
sley called to order, and asked, what had the history of last
winter to do with the Constitution. Several gentlemen, and among
the rest the Hon. Mr. Adams, said the gentleman was in order—
let him go on in his own way.] I am going, Mr. President, to
show you, my brother farmers, what were the effects of anarchy,
that you may see the reasons why I wish for good government.

* J. Elliott (ed.), *Debates in the Several State Conventions on the
Adoption of the Federal Constitution,* 2nd ed., 4 vols. (Washington, 1836), II, 118–120.

People say I took up arms; and then, if you went to speak to them, you had the musket of death presented to your breast. They would rob you of your property; threaten to burn your houses; oblige you to be on your guard night and day; alarms spread from town to town; families were broken up; the tender mother would cry, "O, my son is among them! What shall I do for my child!" Some were taken captive, children taken out of their schools, and carried away. Then we should hear of an action, and the poor prisoners were set in the front, to be killed by their own friends. How dreadful, how distressing was this! Our distress was so great that we should have been glad to snatch at any thing that looked like a government. Had any person, that was able to protect us, come and set up his standard, we should all have flocked to it, even if it had been a monarch; and that monarch might have proved a tyrant;—so that you see that anarchy leads to tyranny, and better have one tyrant than so many at once.

Now, Mr. President, when I saw this Constitution, I found that it was a cure for these disorders. It was just such a thing as we wanted. I got a copy of it, and read it over and over. I had been a member of the Convention to form our own state constitution, and had learnt something of the checks and balances of power, and I found them all here. I did not go to any lawyer, to ask his opinion; we have no lawyer in our town, and we do well enough without. I formed my own opinion, and was pleased with this Constitution. My honorable old daddy there [pointing to Mr. Singletary] won't think that I expect to be a Congressman, and swallow up the liberties of the people. I never had any post, nor do I want one. But I don't think the worse of the Constitution because lawyers, and men of learning, and moneyed men, are fond of it. I don't suspect that they want to get into Congress and abuse their power. I am not of such a jealous make. They that are honest men themselves are not apt to suspect other people. I don't know why our constituents have not a good right to be as jealous of us as we seem to be of the Congress; and I think those gentlemen, who are so very suspicious that as soon as a man gets into power he turns rogue, had better look at home.

We are, by this Constitution, allowed to send ten members to Congress. Have we not more than that number fit to go? I dare say, if we pick out ten, we shall have another ten left, and I hope ten times ten; and will not these be a check upon those that go? Will they go to Congress, and abuse their power, and do mischief, when they know they must return and look the other ten in the face, and be called to account for their conduct? Some gentlemen think that our liberty and property are not safe in the hands of moneyed men, and men of learning? I am not of that mind.

Brother farmers, let us suppose a case, now: Suppose you had a farm of 50 acres, and your title was disputed, and there was a farm of 5000 acres joined to you, that belonged to a man of learning, and his title was involved in the same difficulty; would you not be glad to have him for your friend, rather than to stand alone in the dispute? Well, the case is the same. These lawyers, these moneyed men, these men of learning, are all embarked in the same cause with us, and we must all swim or sink together; and shall we throw the Constitution overboard because it does not please us alike? Suppose two or three of you had been at the pains to break up a piece of rough land, and sow it with wheat; would you let it lie waste because you could not agree what sort of a fence to make? Would it not be better to put up a fence that did not please every one's fancy, rather than not fence it at all, or keep disputing about it until the wild beasts came in and devoured it? Some gentlemen say, Don't be in a hurry; take time to consider, and don't take a leap in the dark. I say, Take things in time; gather fruit when it is ripe. There is a time to sow and a time to reap; we sowed our seed when we sent men to the federal Convention; now is the harvest, now is the time to reap the fruit of our labor; and if we won't do it now, I am afraid we never shall have another opportunity.

VAN NOSTRAND REINHOLD ANVIL BOOKS